The Fighting Rifle book 1

The Fighting Rifle, Volume 1

Mike Harland

Published by Mike Harland, 2021.

The Fighting Rifle
Book 1

Book 1 of ITC rifle training

The Fighting Rifle
Book 1

Dedication
To my family who have always been supportive
of all my endeavors
And all those who serve righteousness with
love and perseverance

About The Author

I was trained for 16-17 years in Karate, reaching black belt 2nd Dan in 1991. During this period, I participated in a number of karate competitions, winning gold and a number of bronze medals in competition. From 1985-1986 did my national service in the South African Defense Force (SADF), doing border duty for 9 months in the combat area (red zone/war zone). As a 20-year-old I saw my first contact (real life shooting) as a group of ANC/ SWAPO terrorist organizations attacked our base. Although it was probably SWAPO as the ANC's "Spear of the nation" army was a bit blunt and lost every contact with SA forces.

From about 1987 till the early 90's I worked doing door duty at clubs. During this period in our country, badly behaved people normally took their punishment like a man, and that was where I had most of my street experience situations up until about 40 years of age. Personally, and in the capacity of a soldier and Close Protection Specialist I have used pistols and rifles extensively.

People mostly want to know what you based your training on and what experience you have. It is good for someone to ask because their life depends on the training they will receive from an instructor. You need to know that the person who is teaching you actually has experience in real combat. What does the person teaching you have to draw from as an instructor if he has no experience? Without a penchant for training in combat you won't have the will to succeed – you need a certain disposition that predisposes you to this.

In 1992 I developed an interest in Close Protection (CP), which was a very new occupation in the public sector in South Africa at the time. There was not much in the way of sophisticated training courses for civilians. So whenever there was a possibility to train with an instructor that knew what he was talking about, we would jump at the opportunity. During the period 1992 till 2005 I attended 4 separate CP courses and a number of other related courses such as shooting in low light, advanced foot and vehicle drills, Improvised Explosive Devices (IED) recognition, unarmed combat, knife fighting, and numerous other skills and courses not mentioned here. These instructors ranged from civilian instructors to ex Special Forces (SF) and FBI certified instructors. During my CP experience, I have looked after celebrities, businessmen, royalty and diplomats.

I was able to apply IED recognition experience in counter terrorism operations. In 2000 I was tasked to come up with a plan to minimize IEDs being placed in The V&A Waterfront Cape Town.

South Africa has a tradition of hunters and shooters because of the nature of the land and its tumultuous history over the last 300 years, where hunting and fighting were the order of the day, and this gave most South Africans a good taste of reality in combat. Therefore, it was more likely that we would be exposed to weapons living in South Africa.

In the military we dealt with all sorts of weapons and equipment, such as radar and radio communications etc. High threat CP is commonly referred to as Private Security Detail (PSD), and during 2004 the conflict in Iraq attracted a lot of PSD operators from all over the world. Having military experience and about 15 years in CP by that time, I decided it would benefit my overall abilities to get some PSD experience and training.

You soon learn it takes a determined, focused and deliberate mindset balanced with self confidence that will allow you to win in a real gunfight; there is no room for negative thoughts or thoughts that detract from the winning, orientated and focused mind.

When you train for combat in reality it helps to train instinctively and to train so you react and don't have to think about tactics because there is only time for reacting.

My experience with martial and unarmed combat spans about 38 years where I trained not just with Karate systems but also to a minor degree Aikido (which is not a self-defense system), Judo and some ground fighting. My weapons training was with various weapon systems, handguns and rifles etc. which spans about 30 years.

To better understand where my skill level was in terms of international standards, I did an advanced certificate in handgun and rifle skills to round off my weapons qualifications. This certifies a person to teach to an advanced level anywhere in the world and is internationally recognized. From approximately 1994/97 I started to develop the mobility shooting drills for handgun and rifle which you can now see on YouTube and also on Patreon see below.

During this period, I got most of my Close Protection experience and was tasked as team leader about 70 times or more. In the period 1990-1991 I studied physical education which has helped me better understand the body and how it functions. I apply this in my unarmed combat and weapons training courses.

Overview Of This Training Manual

The subject matter is the use of a semi-automatic rifle in a combat environment or military, SHTF environment, and will also refer to Personal Defense Weapons (PDWs) as they have roughly the same format.

This manual focuses primarily on the **combative** use of semi auto rifles, not *marksmanship* per se. You can take basic shooting courses with instructors who teach the finer aspects of using e.g., a 1-point rifle sling versus a 2 or even 3 point sling. They focus on marksmanship aspects like different skills for e.g., transitioning a rifle from target to target, or advanced recoil management. I prefer to train students and focus on the combative aspect of firearm techniques. Yes, you need solid fundamental marksmanship skills, and you develop those when training anyway. What many students (and instructors) lack, is a better understanding of **actual fighting techniques** with firearms, in this case semi auto rifles.

Semi auto rifles that shoot rifle caliber rounds are designated as "carbines", in shooting circles it seems that rifles that shoot pistol rounds can also be referred to as pistol caliber carbine or PDW.

A semi auto rifle with a full-length barrel such as a M16 with an 18- or 19-inch barrel will give you a slight bit more velocity and therefore slight bit more range and impact on target, having better terminal ballistics than a M16 with a 12- or 14-inch barrel.

The assault rifle M4/AK/SIG commando (small caliber rifle ammunition) is a short version of a full-size semi auto rifle/full auto (military) (e.g., FN SIG G3), shooting full powered rifle ammunition. The pistol cartridge caliber short carbine is sometimes called a PDW (personal defense weapon). This could be anything from 9mm to 45 ACP in caliber; mostly the barrel length will be about 8-14 inches or a slight longer.

We will mostly cover drills, techniques and tactics for a single operator but we also touch on tactics for small teams to a lesser extent, as the focus of the manual is **personal defense** with a semi auto rifle.

Training Objectives

The manual attempts to teach the student the handling of a semi auto rifle as well as basic tactical application and procedures. This type of weapon is what would be used on a Close Protection assignment, normally in a high threat environment, or on a larger property than just a house. It is also the best weapon for farm protection because of its capacity, accuracy, relatively light weight and can reach out to a reasonable range of 200 to 300 meters.

This manual is ***not*** a comprehensive list of techniques and tactics about rifle use and is only a guide of the techniques and tactics that will make you a good shooter for combat. To make a complete manual for rifle discipline would make the manual too long. The nuances of combat with a semi auto rifle can only be addressed in person, on a course. Each subject is dealt with in a brief summary to give you an idea of training for the rifle; it's not an exhaustive list of techniques or equipment.

Advanced Versus Basic Skills

Advanced level skill is not always about more tactics or techniques but the improvement in basic skills that allows the shooter to shoot at a higher level. Improving your grip, fast target acquisition, use of cover, shooting moving targets and your lateral and other movements will improve your overall ability. This will make you "king of the battlefield", **not techniques or shooting positions that you will never use in a realistic battle.**

The basic level student is not only determined by the number of techniques they can do but by **how they perform the techniques they know. The advanced level student is expected to have superior awareness and skills developed from hours of repetition.** The few advanced techniques you might learn on an advanced operator training course won't necessary mean victory in a combat environment.

For an illustration let's say a person has 3 weeks to do the full course from basic to advanced but has not had the time to integrate the techniques into their **subconscious mind.** This means the techniques they learnt can only be done at a very **slow pace.** An **advanced student** can do all the techniques the same as the person with 3 weeks training but can do them at a **faster** pace and **can integrate (doing 3 or more techniques simultaneously)** them as well. Such as doing accurate well aimed shots on targets, while moving then perform a magazine change and do remedial action in the event of a stoppage. That sort of level is what will separate the advanced shooter from a basic shooter.

From experience I would say a person that has trained mainly weapon presentation and has ingrained it to a subconscious level and can shoot accurately under stress will beat any person who has done the most advanced rifle course in the world but hasn't internalized the material, because without the movement being subconscious and fluid without thought will mean it will take conscious thought which will slow them down and this could lead to their death in a fight.

Structure Of This Manual

We'll begin by looking at a basic history of combat rifles, then cover numerous aspects of modern rifles and auxiliary equipment. Thereafter we'll look at the nature of combat, relevant mental performance, and training techniques suitable for combative rifles. The remainder of the manual then describes a range of techniques and training exercises for semi auto rifles, ranging from beginner to advanced level.

General Introduction To The Semi Auto Rifle

The following information is not meant to be precise or historically accurate, it's just a guide on how sidearm developed from bolt action rifles to semi auto rifles and submachine guns or PDW (personal defense weapon) and then light PDW like the S&B pistol with brace. The powder developments and metallurgy allowed lighter and compact weapons and the explosion caused by black powder was replaced with smokeless powder that burns slower and gives a longer slow push on the bullet.

In 1884, Paul Vieille **invented** a **smokeless powder** called Poudre B. This means that rifles have only been using smokeless powder for roughly about 140 years. This is not very long in the bigger scheme of things and therefore the technology to actually use the powder effectively has lowly improved over these 140 years and so have the techniques and tactics to go with the technological advances. For example, single action rifles using smokeless powder such as the trap door types used by US cavalry and British. And the bolt action rifles such as the *Mauser with its legendary bolt action*, then onto semi auto rifles such as MP44 (see picture below) used and designed near end of World War 2 (WW2) by the Germans (this was the first proper assault rifle) with an intermediary cartridge 7.92x33 caliber. This only gives us from WW2 till today to develop tactics and techniques to use these new weapons systems, about 80 years, and this is why the correct use and application of the semi auto rifle is still being developed and will be improved over the next 50 to 100 years as people learn the best techniques and tactics for these modern rifles.

One of the reasons it takes long to learn to use the weapon system correctly is because people still have the old mindset of set-piece battles where they think of groups of men facing each other and engaging at medium to close range. It then got a bit more dynamic in WW2 but it was still large groups of men sometimes facing each other in trenches, or across fields where the artillery could bombard them when the enemy location was identified. Another reason is government bureaucracy and the military mindset doesn't change very easily because of tradition, and humans have the propensity to keep things the same.

This applies to almost everything, which is why if you are tailing someone, for instance, and you lose them then you can either go to the entrance of the complex where they came in and they will more than likely come through there again or just go back to their vehicle. This also applies to tailing by vehicle – you can wait on the route and they will more than likely pass there again. This is due to habit that all humans are subject to. That's why trained people leave by another door and Special Forces operators don't go back the same route they infiltrated into an area with.

The improvements in full auto rifle calibers also made a huge difference with weapons such as the MG42 (this is classed as a light machine gun, the acronym being LMG) which could lay down suppressive fire over a front of about 50 to 100 meters that made it difficult for a group of men to travel over the ground. Some of the new innovations have taken the large bulky semi auto rifles in calibers like 308 (7.62x51mm) where they made them shorter and lighter such as "bull pup" designs in 308 calibers. Large volumes of fire mean wear and tear on barrels and this meant a learning curve in the production of barrels to increase barrel life such as cold hammer forged barrels and then came chrome lined barrels (a recent development that I am aware of), and this volume of fire could increase and allowed armies to use LMGs to suppress areas that would make it difficult for opposing armies to move over any open ground.

The next innovation would be to use light but strong materials like polymers in construction of handguns and submachine guns such as the famous MP5 which is all steel except for the hand guard and parts of the body (see below). The next progression as I see it would be something like the B&T with a brace (see below); this is both light and compact and can be braced for slightly more accurate fire than a handheld pistol.

Probably the first submachine gun is what the Germans called the MP18, or the Bergmann Muskete. This weapon was first issued in 1918, the last year of World War I. This was a pistol caliber weapon with full auto capability for military use. One of the earliest semi auto pistols with large military production and use would be the Broom Handel Mauser C96; it had a 10-round capacity and a bullet that travelled at approximately 1350-1400 fps (feet per second).

The semi auto rifle is used in a high threat environment because it has range, penetration and capacity that a pistol does not have (full auto rifles are used for military operation). Most have an effective range of 300 to 500 (depending on bullet selection, barrel length and caliber) meters in 5, 5.6 caliber and in 7.62x51 platform with good shooters able to put a bullet on a man-sized target out to 1000 meters with a standard battle rifle in 7.62x51 caliber. Average effective range was 600 to 800 meters.

SMGs (submachine gun, shorter barrel e.g., 5-8inch barrel which is basically the same as what is called a PDW now) strike a balance between pistol caliber carbine and a battle rifle. An example is the MP5, with an affective range of approximately 100 meters to 150 meters. The battle rifle normally has an effective range of about 300-500 meters, and for 7,62x51 out to 800 meters. The velocity from an 8-inch barrel for pistol caliber carbine is approximately 1300 to 1400, feet per second depending on the type of ammunition, weight of projectile and powder charge used.

The most important aspect to my mind in having a pistol caliber SMG/PDW is that it is easier to suppress an opponent and this is essential in low intensity warfare, also known as SHTF. This is essential when wanting to come to a silent solution to sentry dispatching or noisy early warning OP (observation post). Making noise in an environment where you are trying to be quiet is very important in a lot of combat situations when you are trying to be unobserved. This basically applies to any situation when you are fighting on your own.

The FN P90 uses a lot of polymers, this makes it very light and it is a PDW, but it is very hard to get bullets for it as they're specific to the P90 only. This might not be the case for long though.

The Russian 7.62x54mm cartridge has a range of approximately 600-800 meters using a platform such as a Dragunov/SVD semi auto sniper system, designed in the 60's. The French FN Herstal (Fabrique Nationale) was designed in about the 50's and could also be mounted with a scope and was also fairly accurate as a semi auto sniper system. These weapons are a bit bulky and you can carry limited rounds because of the weight and size of the bullets and the weight and size of the weapons. In roughly the same period the G3, which is the German battle rifle was manufactured.

The Russian 7.62x39mm has an approximate range of 300 to 500 (some say 200-300 max) meters, and if you are an above average shooter then more than 500 meters depending on the weapon e.g., such as RPK that has a longer barrel than the standard AK. For these, use Russian or Czech made ammo, as it is more reliable than ammunition made in the Middle East (use locally manufactured if you are operating in Iraq or Afghanistan).

The AK47, or AK for short, is based on the German MP 44 and the weapons such as the Galil or R4, R5 and R6 (as they're called in South Africa) are a copy of the AK but are very reliable and more accurate than the AK type weapon. This is as a result of the AK being made from pressed steel and the Galil and R4 from machined steel which is more robust and just as reliable in sandy environments (but they are heavier by almost a kilogram). This accuracy is not very obvious as the skill of the operator is a major factor and the distance the weapon is being used at will dictate the overall effectiveness.

The AR15 / M4 / M16 is light and reasonably reliable, but not as reliable as the AK family weapons in a sandy environment, as you will have to make sure an M4 or AK is kept clean. The AK is sometimes used by SF to blend in with local militia e.g., Israeli SF use the Uzi, Galil, M4 and probably variants of the Tavor etc., SA SF use R5, AK 47, M4, MP5 and Russian SF use all AK variants. The AK has been used in a combat environment for a number of years (60 -70 years). Weapons that are based on the outer looks of the M4 but work on different internal mechanism closer to that of the AK that make them more reliable include the H&K 416. Weapons for combat are also made by LWRC (Land Warfare Resources Corporation). They have a variety of short barreled rifles in 5.56mm using gas piston system as well, like the 416.

Sig Sauer make a new range of full and semi auto rifles. The Sig commando (5.56x45mm) is used in Iraq by some PSD companies but it has not got a combat proven record yet that I am aware of, as it is a new model. It would be illogical to use an unproven weapon system in a real-life conflict. All equipment must be tested beforehand. You can be fairly certain some weapon manufacturers like Sig or H&K will work well most of the time.

The best weapon for an individual is the weapon they are used to using and has the most experience with in a decent caliber. Because when it hits the fan, they need to shoot and move instinctively. Make sure the weapon you end up using has ***parts that are available*** "in country" and get the same weapon which you are used to using. It's a bad situation if you cannot get the exact weapon you are used to. You need to know how to do ***basic maintenance*** on your weapon; you need have an ***intimate understanding of your sights,*** whether it's a scope or iron sights.

Your ***weapon slings*** need to be at the correct length and the type that allows you the freedom to shoot and move and then change to pistol or blade. Hopefully the weapon system ***is light enough*** to carry long distance, it needs to be ***robust and doesn't break easily*** which is why the AK is so popular for any type military combat or SHTF type situation.

For convoys and general vehicle operations, have at least one long-range weapon per vehicle so you can "reach out" to far targets. Tried and tested weapons are the H&K G3 in 7.62x51 or 5.56 caliber, FN, SIG, M4 and, Galil 7.62x 51 or 5,56 x45, Steyr AUG etc. It is important to always test the system you will be using in a SHTF or military application. A good procedure would be to use something that has already been tested and is being used by a military.

The longer the history of use the more you can assess the system's reliability and robustness. Most of the time, the initial testing and use of the bull pup battle rifle for the British army gave a lot of problems as did the first M16s issued in Vietnam to US troops.

This image shows Mauser rifles used by Boers in 1900 when Britain attacked South Africa for its gold and diamonds. The Mauser was chambered in 7x57mm cartridges:

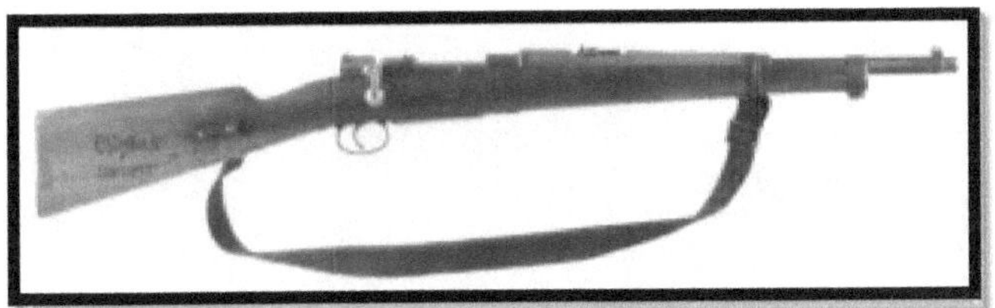

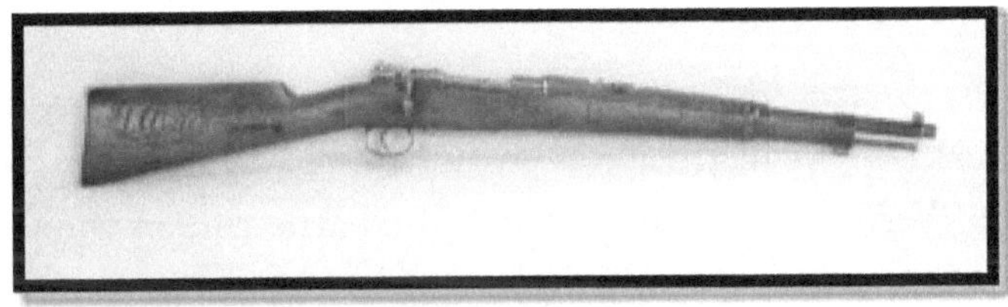

MP 44 (7.92 x33) "Kurtz" (means "short" in German) was the **first proper assault rifle:**

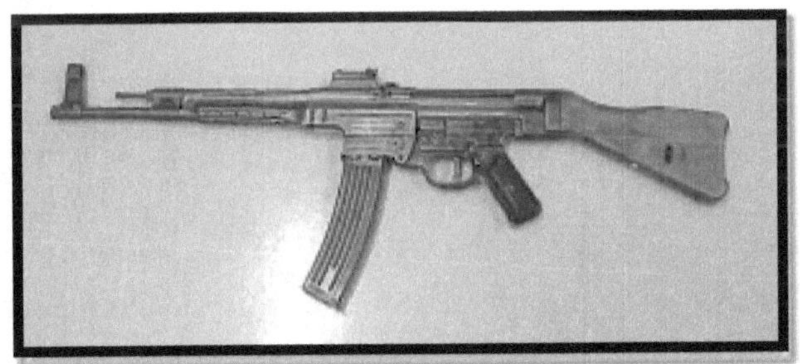

AK 47 7.62x39 (second assault rifle supposedly designed by Kalashnikov; as you can see it's just a copy of the MP44):

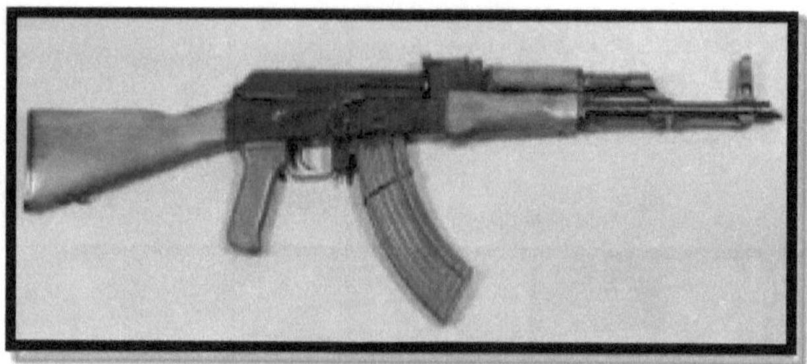

Galil 5,56x45 (the AK was copied by the Israelis to make what they called their IMI Galil then was manufactured by South Africa and designated Vector R4, so they copied the battle rifle of the Germans which was the MP44, via copying the AK)

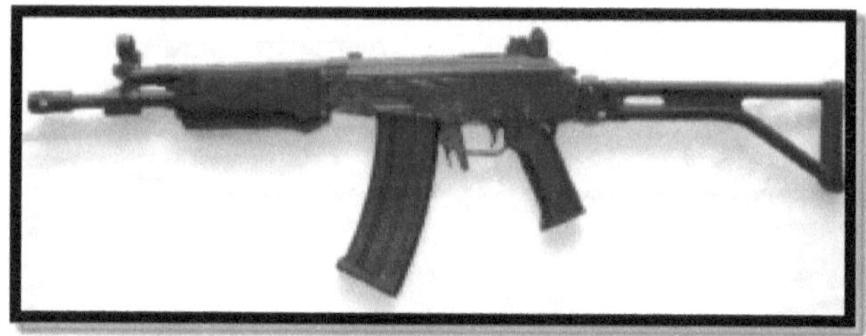

FN 7.62x51 has a much larger caliber and has more energy down range and is therefore not affected by the wind as much as the lighter 5.56x45. It also allows you to penetrate obstacles more easily (a soft tree of 12 inches in diameter is not necessarily a good piece of cover). These rifles have proved very popular in Southern Africa warfare due to these long range and penetrating capabilities:

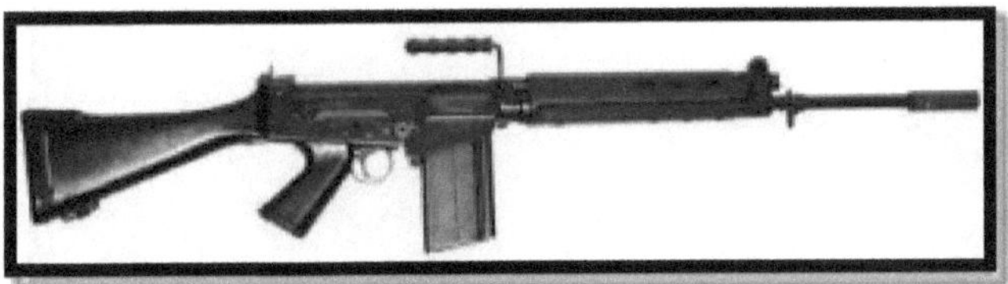

In Southern Africa, the FN is also popular for anti-poaching use. It is fairly reliable if kept clean. Here I am using it on an anti-poaching course:

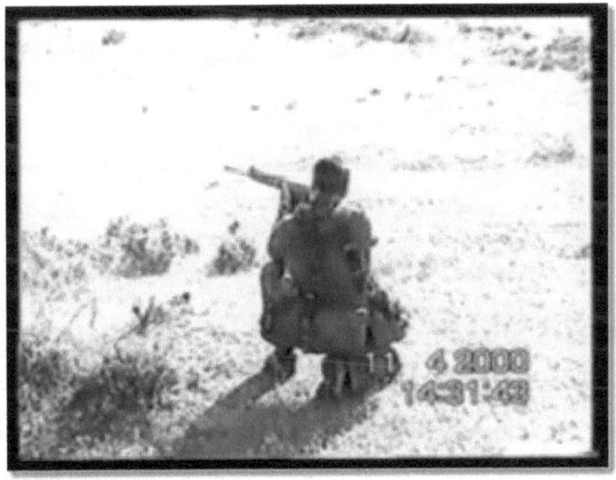

Early Bergmann Semi auto pistol 1910, probably a precursor to the machine gun:

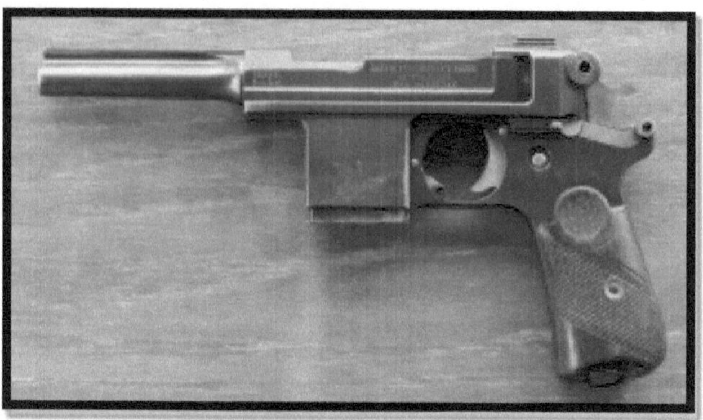

Bergmann Muskete MP18 designed 1916 (original submachine gun or you could also say the original PDW):

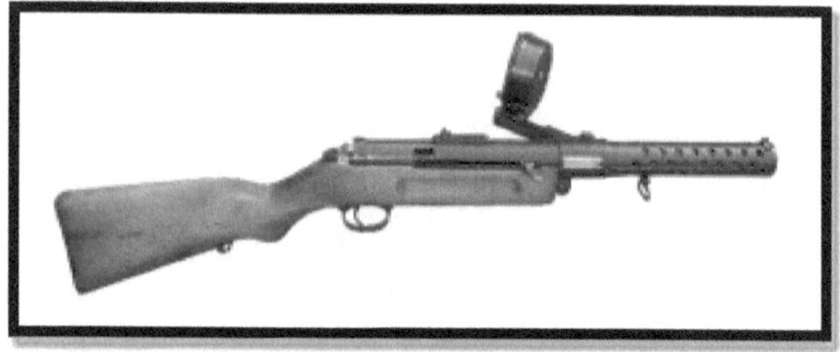

Here are more modern (submachine guns) also designated PDW (Personal Defense Weapon). Most will be or can come in 9 x19 caliber, 40cal or 45cal pistol caliber rounds

CZ Scorpion:

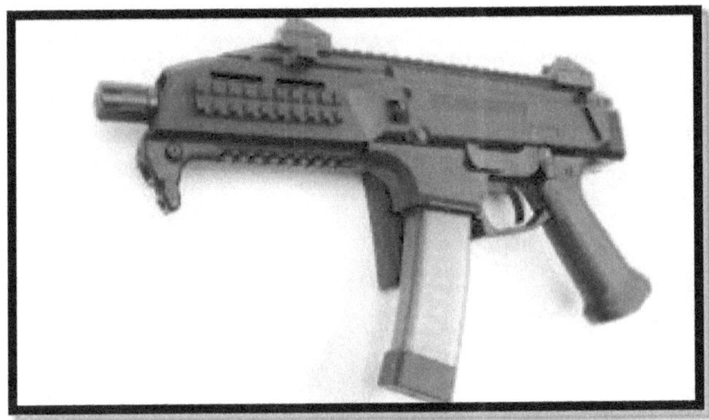

Striborg:

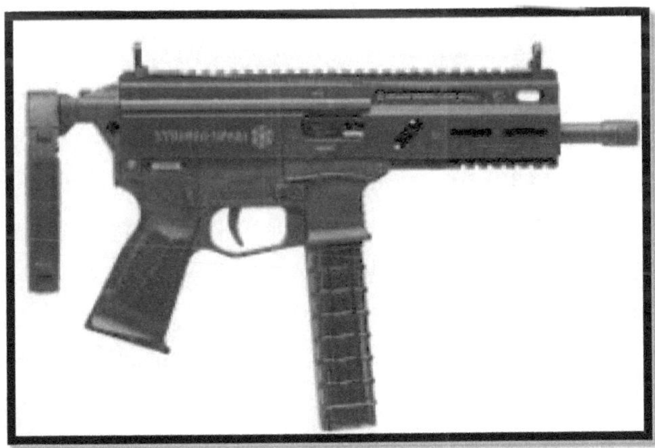

Here is a clone of the MP5 (classic weapon used by anti-terrorism units). This is a reliable and well tested weapon which is used by many special forces around the world as it's proven reliable and durable. It works well suppressed and is accurate due to the delayed roller lock system. It would be a reliable secondary weapon in any SHTF scenario or war. Its application would be more for close recce and certain situations where you need quiet and effective fire power:

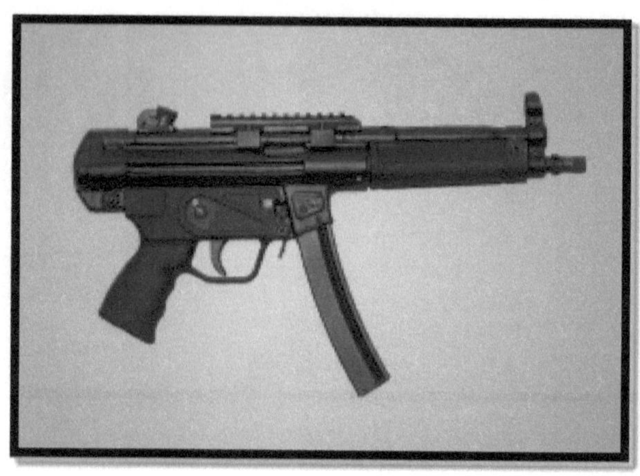

The B&T pistol (this is a fairly recent development in pistol world) offers you a concealable and light option to carry. I am not sure of the reliability as I have not tested it myself, but if it's a reliable and robust shooting platform then it would make a good piece of gear for any type of low threat or SHTF situation. For any military or SHTF situation, going light and fast is essential in any situation where your duty might be recon or maybe where a secondary weapon is needed. As can be seen you can also mount a suppressor with light this gives you the option of going quiet (less sound but not no sound) and target ID at night, very valuable in a house clearing, sentry dispatch, recon function etc. This is therefore a good option for all round security function and if reliable will be a good acquisition.

B&T pistol with brace The same weapon with suppressor

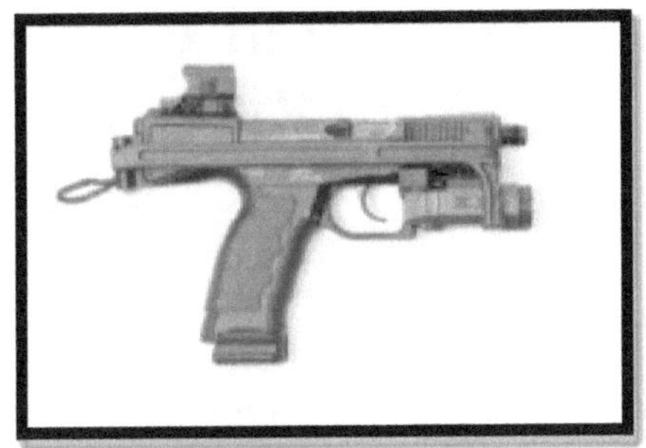

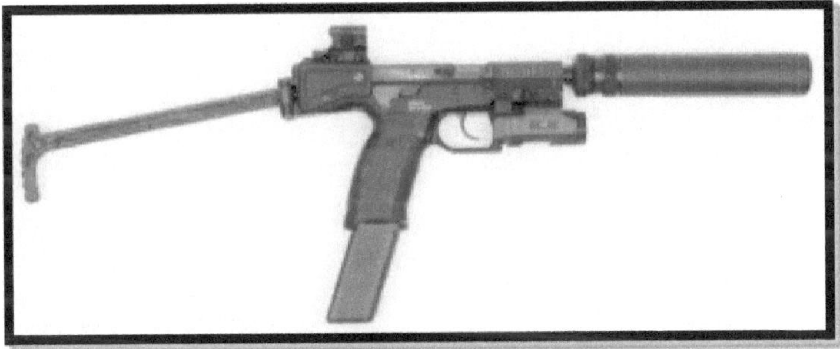

B&T with torch can be used as a light carbine for night operation specially if used with a suppressor:

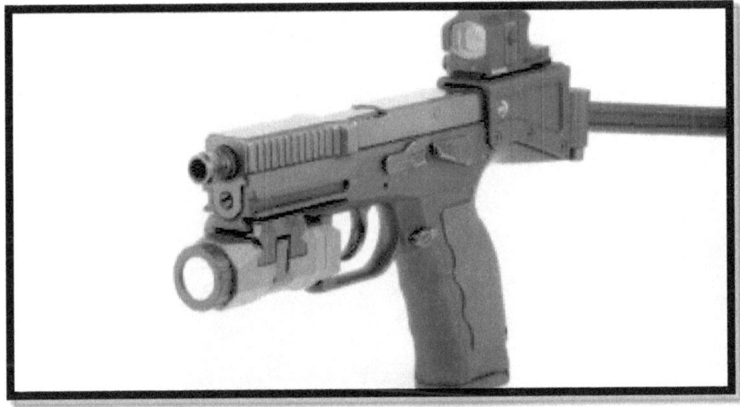

Equipment Associated With The Semi Auto Rifle

The equipment listed and displayed below is not necessarily recommended by me, it's just as a demonstration of what is available to the public. If I recommend a specific piece of equipment, I will state it clearly, as well as what I think of its robustness and functionality if it's been tested by me. It's therefore not an endorsement of a piece of equipment if it is displayed below, it might just be an example.

Cleaning kit

Cleaning kit should be compact for operational use, so it takes up minimal space and can still get the rifle thoroughly clean. This would be especially important when in a prolonged operational environment. Important areas would be gas ports on semi auto rifles which normally requires a gas port reamer or similar (you can make a piece of equipment like this in a pinch but make sure it does the job). Because carrying a cleaning rod is very difficult and unnecessarily heavy as well as awkward to carry, people normally carry a bore snake.

Some rifles (assault/battle/bolt action) have cleaning kits in the butt stock. If this is the case for your weapon system, keep it stocked up whenever possible. This used to be a feature in some older rifles e.g., used in first and second World Wars and later, but is not as a much a feature on modern firearms.

Bore snake: this is a light and effective peace of kit and can be easily carried as seen on the stock here:

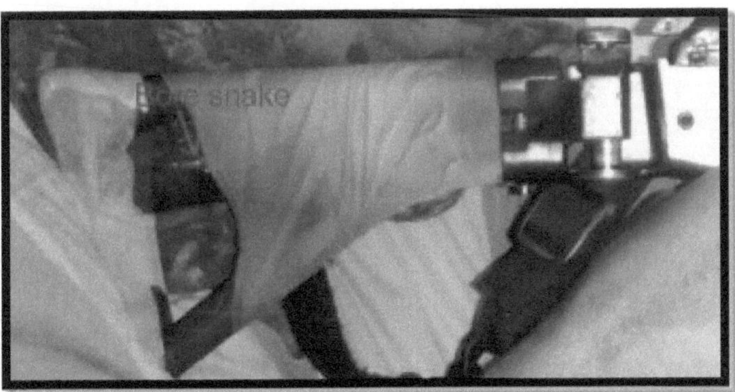

Drop pouch

Drop pouch for empty magazines or any item that you will need later. This normally hangs off your belt at 4 o'clock or 8 o'clock, on the weak side if possible. Some people use it to collect edibles **when not in combat**, the options are up to you, and if you fill it up then it's not going to be useful for dropping magazines in (keep this in mind). I personally don't use one but I can see its benefit in certain situations.

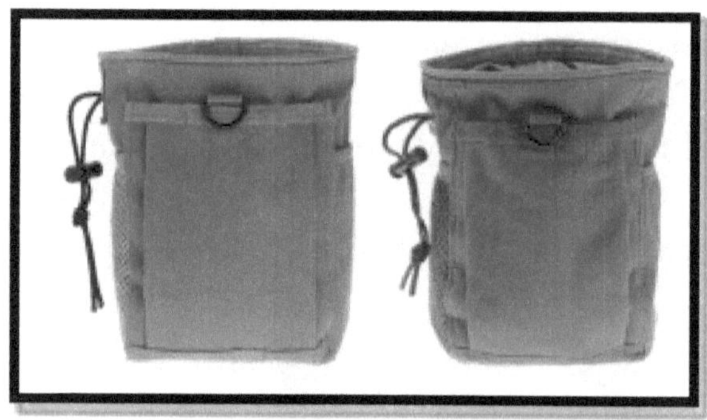

Rifle sling

Rifle sling should be practical and should not hinder the transition from rifle to handgun; it should also keep the weapon from moving too much especially if you will be doing a lot of climbing so you might consider a different sling for combat and another sling for climbing purposes.

1. The normal sling which goes form barrel (fore end of rifle) to stock is ok for general use but for military or high threat use where you will need a sling that keeps the weapon ready at hand. The two-point sling pictured below is good if you are climbing and need the weapon to stay close to your body, though you might have to tighten it to stop it from moving when climbing or running.

2. If you have a clip-on sling that is connected to the back of the rifle by the stock, that allows the weapon to be hung down in front and just needs clipping off when not need or clipped back on, or unclipped when you need to put the weapon down or want to carry in hand. See second picture for example of those below. It's convenient to be able to take the rifle off when doing certain jobs like when having to drive as it's easier to put the rifle aside.

3. If possible, have a sling that will allow you to put the rifle behind you when climbing; it should not hook on magazines or other items. Having said that you will always have the rifle hang up on something, but try minimize this as much as possible. A slick system of magazine holders for your 30 round magazines on the chest can sometimes get in the way and I find to have them lower down near stomach area, but not hindering your forward leaning ability, is a good place to have them. It can be quite a problem getting the right type of sling

and some are useful for climbing and yet others for combat (where accessibility to webbing and equipment is more important).

Examples of rifle slings

Two-point sling will be more stable during climbing and situations where you don't want it to swing around too much. This will not allow a fast response to an attack, but this will mean you will have to use your pistol, or if very close then your blade:

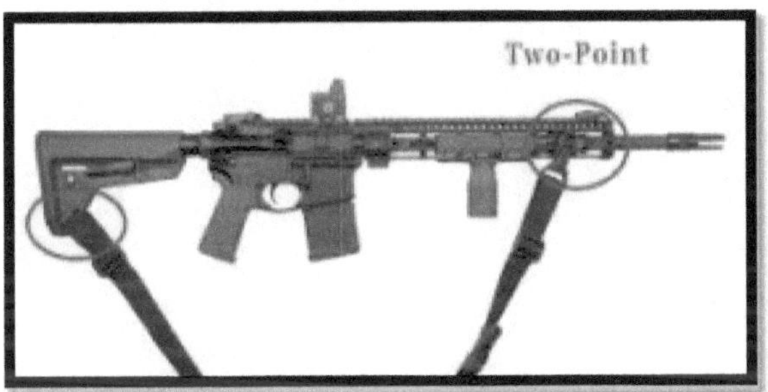

The one-point sling will be easier to get into action as it has less to hook on or get in the way. A clip can also be used to clip the weapon on and off when needed for use when crawling or any other action requiring disengaging the weapon from your body. The example below (with option of increased magnification by using a scope with 1-6-1-8 or 1-10) will also serve you better in a situation where you need the option of close range and medium combat range shooting out to 300 meters.

Single point slings variations are shown below. I personally prefer it close to the pistol grip as this is less likely to allow your barrel to stick in the sand or drag on the ground when kneeling (a suppressor will prevent this from happening to a degree).

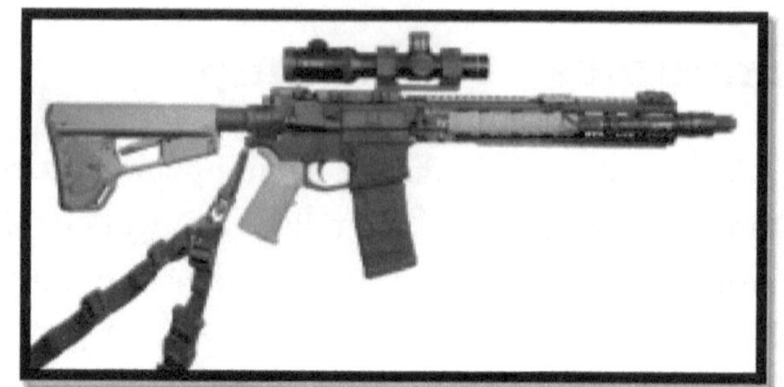

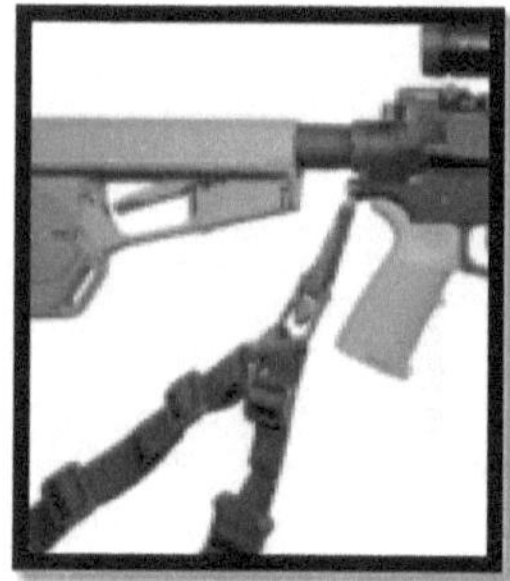

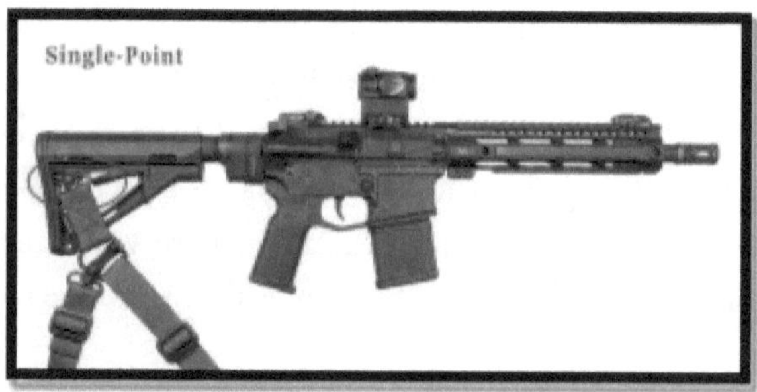
Single-Point

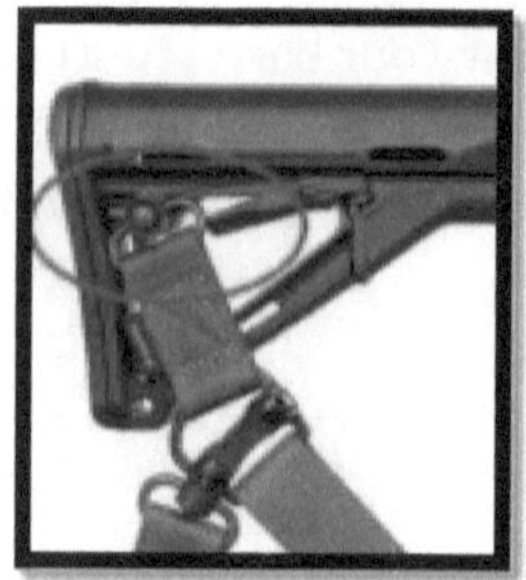

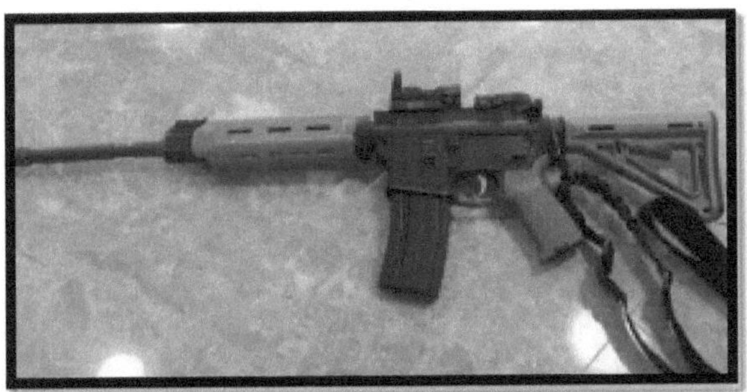

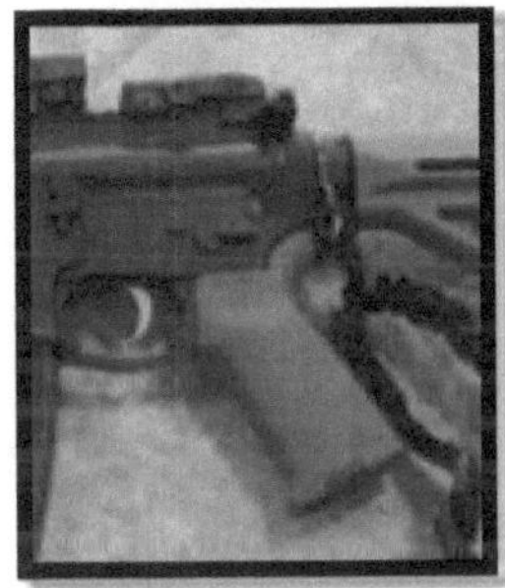

The picture below shows where the single point sling will hang if carried in this way (if you don't have a short stock then a long stock could hit you in the face when squatting). A short stock also helps you when you want to bring it to your centerline for moving through a house or a jungle lane and need to keep the weapon centered and close to the body to facilitate fast turning and easier movement.

When the **stock** is closer to the **centerline** your **movement is more natural** and easier as you are more balanced. Therefore, keep this in mind when you put your sling on and when you decide what length to make the stock (a telescoping stock is very good for this). The sling must not interfere with proper sight alignment, test it so that you can use without getting caught up:

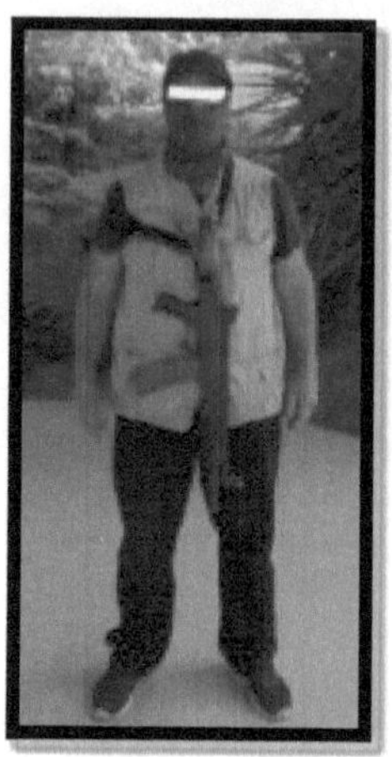

Iron sights

Most semi auto rifles used for military purposes will have iron sights and these I feel are better for all out combat for ruggedness. In military service such sights will do the job for ranges 0 - 200 meters from my experience in the military. This doesn't mean that having a scope isn't better – if you can find a robust enough scope setup, you will have an edge in longer range engagements.

1. Iron sights are not as accurate at longer distances as a good scope. Even a "4 power" scope is fairly good for close range, but iron sights are less likely to give in due to a malfunction. Iron sights don't need batteries and seem to move less than optics and seem to keep their zero quiet well if used, set and maintained correctly.

2. They are fairly foolproof and are a good option for close range battle where reliability is important. It's going to be a tossup between precision and possibly having the optic going off 'point of aim' or coming loose from the rifle body and therefore the ruggedness of iron sights can be very beneficial in battlefield conditions.

3. The way to use these specific sights are to have the rear and front sight *circles match* then line the front post onto a target. Don't tilt your head or put it to the side, keep it close to your centerline, otherwise this will slightly imbalance you. Eye relief is important as depicted below.

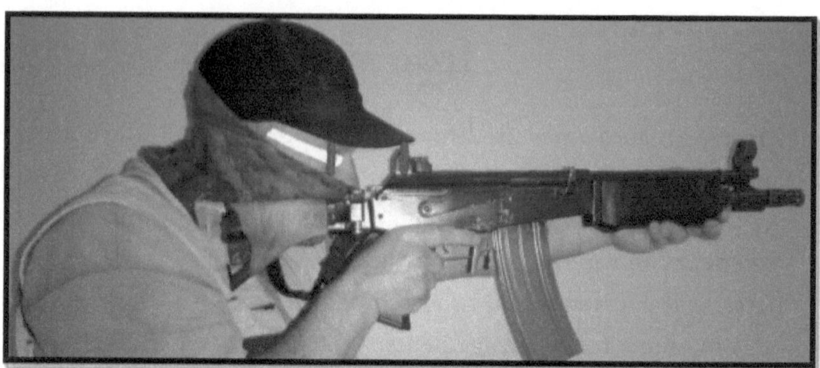

Optical Sights

Scopes or aiming devices are dependent on the operational needs of the shooter and can vary from red dots to magnified scopes. But first test it before using in combat, this is because it needs to be robust and not lose point of aim if bumped. That is why all military scopes go through rigorous testing to be accepted. Keep in mind in combat (military or SHTF) you will very seldom be shooting further than 300 meters.

This does not apply to snipers as they will normally be trying to shoot from 300 m and further, maybe out to 800 meters for a military sniper, as they want both distance from the enemy and to be close enough not to miss. This is because once you miss you are making the target harder to get at next time and you will have failed your mission as well as alerted the enemy to your presence.

"One shot one kill" thinking is mostly a fantasy as very few people can make a 1 shot 1 kill at extended ranges of 800 meters. In some engagements where snipers are working in an area, they will shoot many rounds before a hit on the intended target. This is due to the many variables that are involved in shooting out to ranges past 400 meters.

1. Point aim sights that assist *fast target acquisition* (reflex sights) are for fairly close-range fast shooting such as would be relevant in a combat environment. Such a sight should always be as rugged as possible; the problem will be what can you afford

    a. Red dot type sights are good for intermediate ranges and allow fast target acquisition.

    b. Aim-point make red dot sights and other similar sights for hunting and military use.

    c. Sights with both red dot and magnification are best as they allow fast target acquisition close up and magnification for longer range targets e.g., a scope like IOR Valdada 1-10 which allows a red dot type capacity (there will be slightly more of your view taken up though due to the bulk of the scope).

2. Scopes with zoom capability

    a. Low zoom capability: good choices include ACOG 1-6 for general purpose and the Dragunov also has a 6 magnification for medium to far range, being 400-800m. The rifle capability should dictate the type of scope as you wouldn't put a 6-24 power on a battle rifle because you would have very limited field of view.

    b. Scopes with 1-4 magnification, 1-6, 1-8 or 1-10 will be sufficient for 5.56x45 or 7.62x51 battle rifles. These will give you both field of view and range and accuracy out to about 400 or even 800 meters, depending on your training and knowledge.

    c. Long range scope examples include Leupold, Vortex, IOR Valdada, Leica, Night force etc. with up to 20x magnification. A high magnification will be used on a sniper system due to its long-range effectiveness.

The IOR 1-10 Ghost scope shown here is a good all round versatile one for close and long range applications. Keep in mind I haven't actually tested this scope so I can't give you any advice on whether it is rugged and reliable but the basic specs mean it should perform fairly well in a close to medium range battle space.

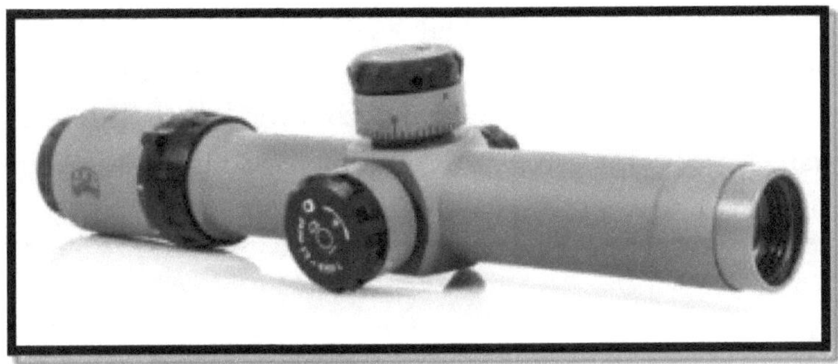

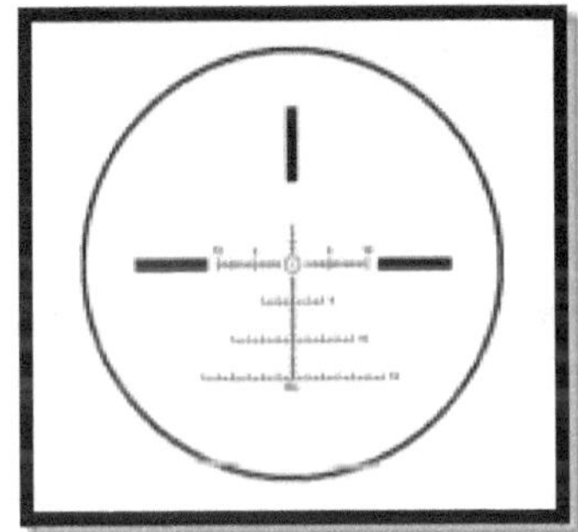

A long-range scope should be appropriate for the caliber you are using for example a 5.56 x 45 caliber rifle has an effective range of about 500 meters (don't stress about max range). This is only a rough estimate, depending on bullet type powder and cartridge and if you want to be pedantic then the air temperature will also affect the outcome so a 1-6/8 or 1-10 will be good enough magnification for your scope.

The 338 Lapua Magnum has a 1500-metre range or slightly more depending on the shooter, therefore a 2-10 or a 3-15 magnification scope would be good enough. The 12.7 Barrett has a 2000- 2500-metre effective range so a scope with 20/30 or 40 magnifications would be good, not so much for the aiming aspect but to be able to see what you are shooting at, in other words identification. These are all dependent on the preference of the shooter, their experience, and requirements for the operation.

The picture below shows a Lapua 338 with scope and a suppressor for sound and flash signature suppression and assisting with negating dust kicking up by the gases escaping from the barrel. This is a good long-range system for "overwatch" and high points where you have a large area to observe and engage the enemy:

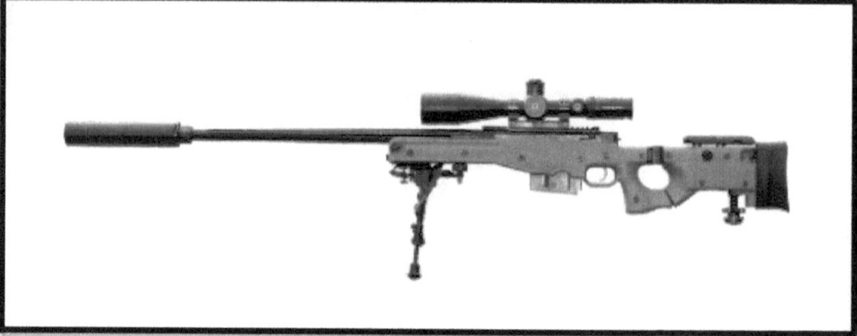

Close Range Scopes

The **Trijicon TA 648 TRD** (shown below) is a close to medium range scope and would be for a military purpose where the ranges are 50-300 meters, ideally for precision out to ranges where the enemy isn't able to exercise the same precision against you. This gives the operator the edge; it also allows the operator to identify the enemy or friend:

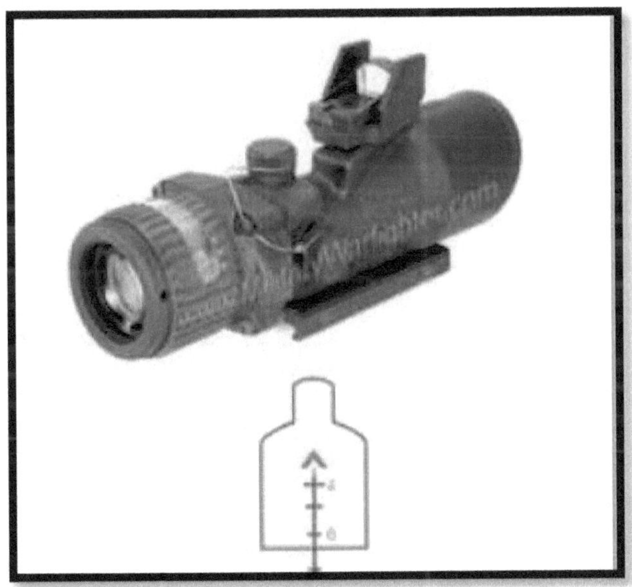

Trijicon electro optics 35 mm thermal weapon sights 8 x s zoom

Thermal is good for night time operations and allows you to engage fairly accurately at night once the scope is set in. A robust scope is very important as a scope that goes out of alignment or loses its focus due to knocks is useless to a military operator or in a SHTF situation:

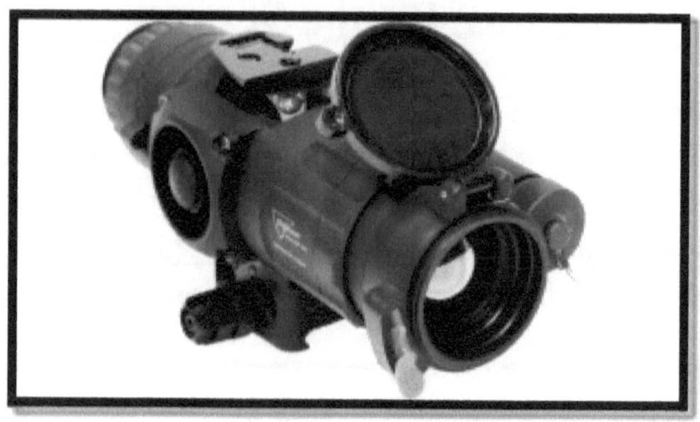

Dangerous game scope

The reticule below will allow fast target acquisition but you will need to dial in the distance and this will take more time than the reticule used above. The reticule below will suit a PDW in a pistol caliber more as it doesn't allow much hold off and is just a fast-aiming option.

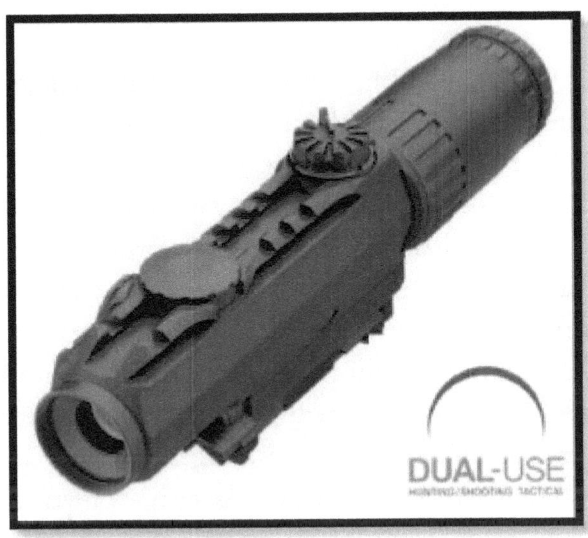
DUAL-USE
HUNTING/SHOOTING TACTICAL

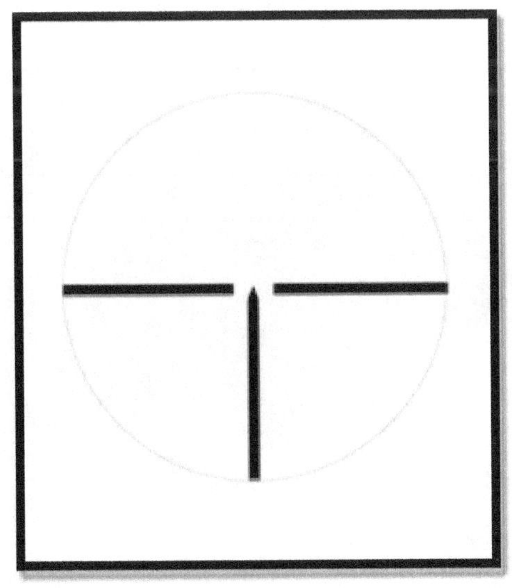

Reflex sight

Reflex sights like the EOTech, Vortex red dot, Aimpoint etc. would be good for your semi auto rifle. If the reticule is illuminated then you have an easy way of seeing the sight and superimposing the dot on the target.

This sight is going to benefit a person who will be shooting fast and at close range with either a PDW or a short carbine rifle in a caliber such as 5.56x45 (9mm or 7.62x39). It will be expedient to be able to see a ***lot of the target and the area*** around the target that you are aiming at, as this allows for fast follow up shots and fast target acquisition. It will be a good addition for night time use if it has an illuminated reticule, but a problem will be to see the actual target as it's not a scope with magnification (and that is why people like to use a thermal imager in such situations). Some thermals have day night options which are ideal. This sight (reflex sight) is very quick to use if the dot is bright enough and the glass is not obscured with mud or dust.

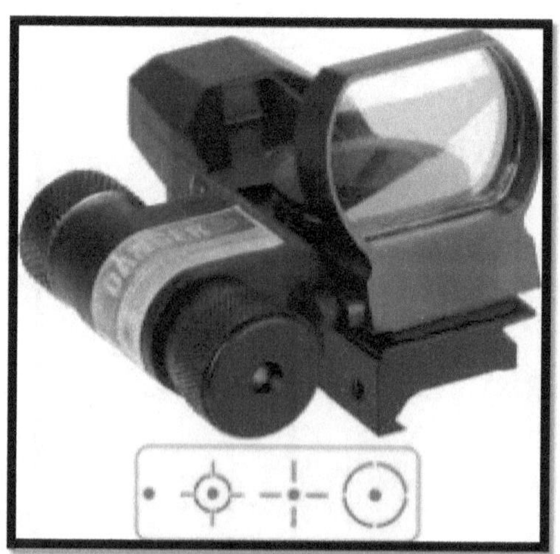

Medium range scopes

At 100m-200m combat shooting in a military role, these scopes are applicable for fast engagements where speed and accuracy are needed. This is due to the fact they allow a better field of view and therefore a better chance at engaging targets more effectively.

Rifles scopes for medium ranges examples include:

1. Kahles K16i (1-6 magnification): this scope is quite expensive though.
2. IOR Valdada (1-10 magnification): expensive, best all round scope for close to medium range (made by a factory that makes military scopes), very robust excellent glass, good reticule. Keep in mind **I haven't tested this scope so it's an opinion** just from looking at the specifications and checking reviews done on the scope.
3. Lynx LX3 (1-6 magnification): reasonable cost and fairly robust.

Kahles scope:

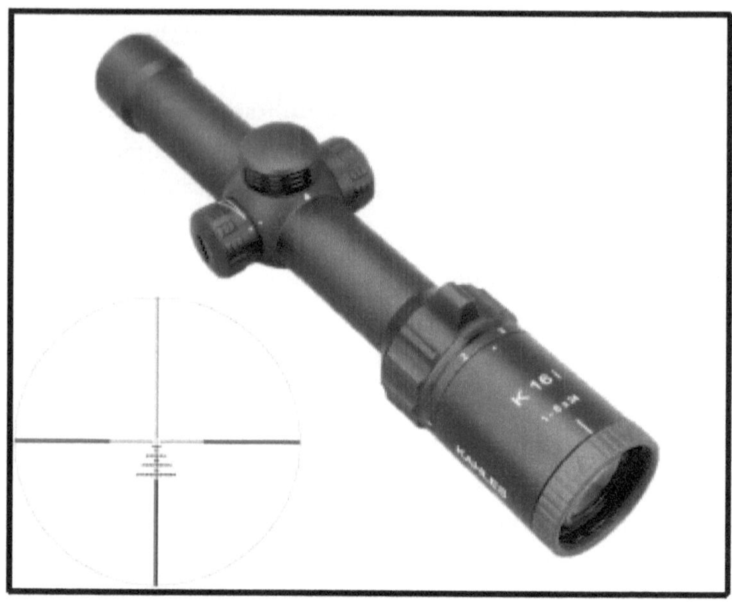

IOR Valdada scope:

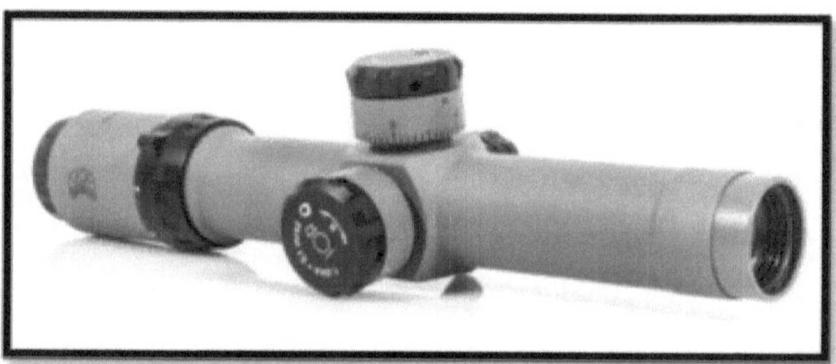

Lynx scope:

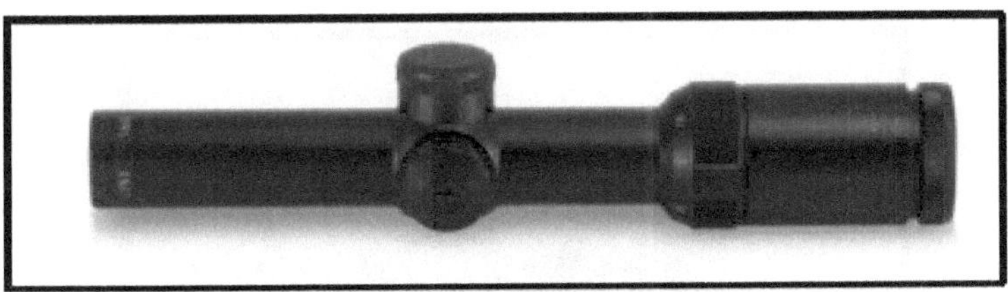

Elcan Specter DR 1-4x:

Keep in mind World War 2 snipers used mostly 4-6 powered scopes and some German units had 8 powered scopes. This reticule below is used by some military units and allows quick target acquisition. Choosing a good reticule for your purposes is important because of the different variations which will suit different purposes. The Elcan looks like it will benefit a user for medium ranges of combat and allow a fairly quick target acquisition and also allow you to hold off using the circle that will correspond to different distances. I would use this scope for rifle cartridges more capable for long range calibers like 5.56x45 and 7.62x51. For fast target acquisition out to longer ranges with a medium caliber semi-auto rifle it helps to have a reticule designed for the bullet and caliber (as some scopes do).

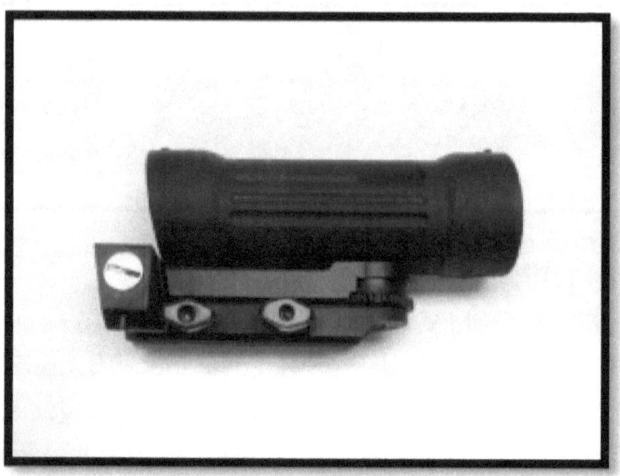

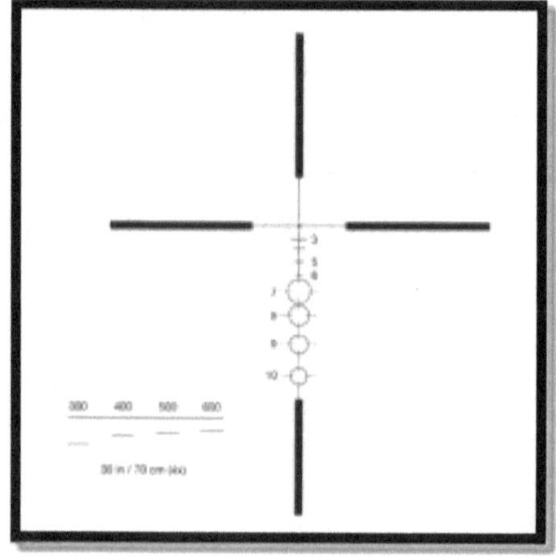
300   400   500   600
98 in / 70 cm (4x)

Rifle bag

Rifle bag must have good padding and or hard outer cover, if possible, for protection. This is to stop the weapon from being damaged when bumped and so that the scope is not affected. This also protects the weapon and scope to a certain extent from the element, like moisture and dirt. For hunting or sniping it could also be fitted with a drag mat at the bottom (side on the ground), sown on to allow for dragging in a situation where a low profile is needed. It should hold at least a cleaning kit, extra magazine, cleaning rod for the barrel, and tools to dismantle the weapon if hunting for a long period or using it in a sniping capacity. Basically, a comprehensive bag for long term hunting trips is ideal; you don't want to leave anything important behind. Have all the correct associated gear (cleaning kit etc.) This will ensure that it works and gives you accuracy out in the field:

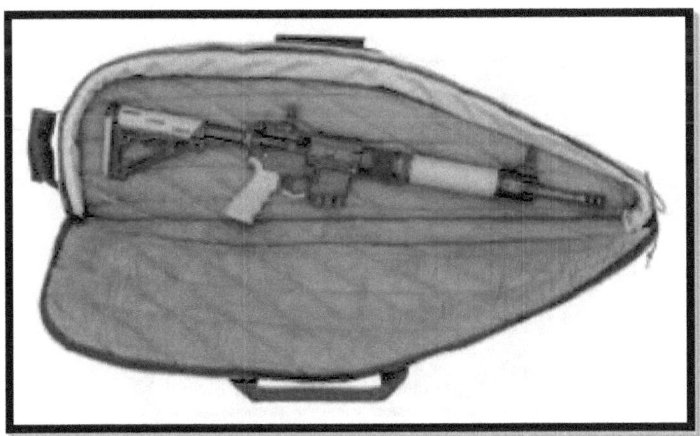

Laser rangefinder

Laser rangefinder and other aiming aids are less likely to be use by Personal Security Detail (PSD) and other Close Protection (CP) teams because they do not normally move at night in certain context when operating in high threat environments such as the Middle East. Having said that, one of the tactics is to move at night when having to take a convoy to an area that is ***very dangerous*** during the day, but this is not the norm, that I am aware of. This is because of the dangers of driving at night and to add to this the civilian protectors would most likely not have night vision, unless they brought them from military ex operators that had access to such devices or from a country that is fairly sophisticated to where a Special Forces unit can access such devices. These devices can be used in PSD operations with operators in static positions where they need to laser the range to a target for precision shooting:

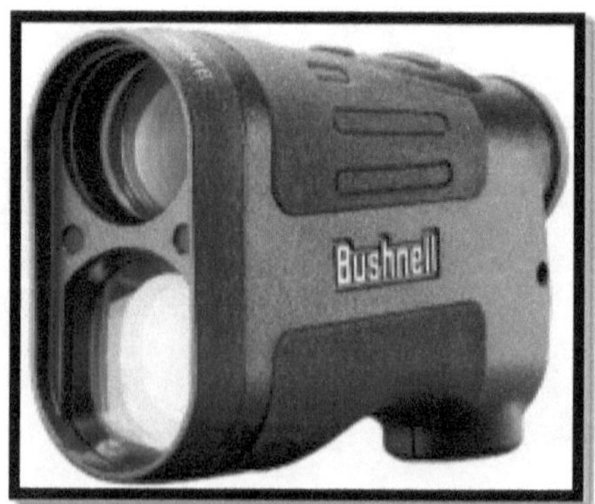

Weapon mounted lasers

Weapon mounted lasers could be more useful for hunting and PSD operations as well as some military operations, because it assists with fast target acquisition in low light. This would be an added benefit for combat in a low light shooting scenario. It would be more appropriate to use a passive laser in a military type scenario as you would not want the enemy to shoot where they see the laser emanating from.

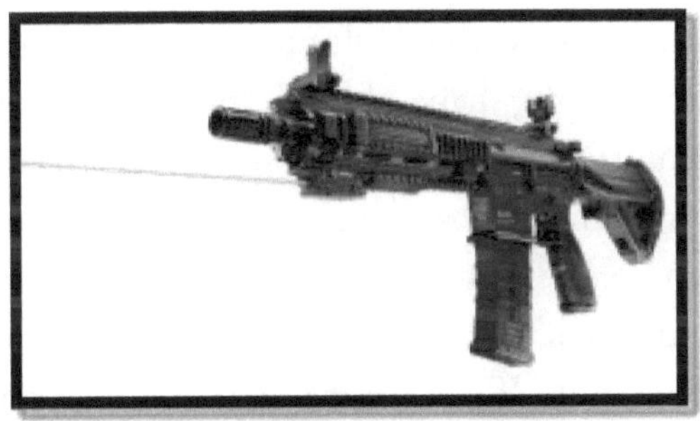

Camouflage for a rifle

Before camouflaging a rifle, you will need to degrease it first. Camouflage for a rifle is normally used on sniper systems or for SF operators during reconnaissance operations. This is a combination of strips of material (called "scrim") and paint in form of spray for sniper systems and *for reconnaissance* purposes they *may only use paint.* Scrim can sometimes hook on any plant, thorns or brush and give you away when close to the enemy (use any paint that sticks to gun metal, make sure its compatible with oil). It's more appropriate to use vertical lines to break up the long shape of the (typically) black weapon. Keep in mind it's going to wear off fairly quickly if it isn't a good quality spray paint. If in doubt, choose a weapon with a base color of "coyote tan" or use a tan color spray paint as this will be a good background color then add stripes of brown (depending on terrain); green and grey are a good combination. If you want to add scrim as you see on some sniper systems then make sure it doesn't stop the mechanism of the rifle working.

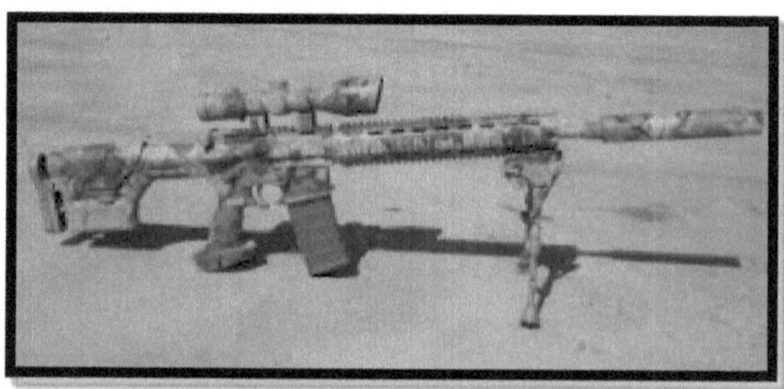

Suppressors for your semi auto rifle

These are not just for the sound suppression but also to take the signature of the flash down considerably when shooting in low light situations especially. For communication you need to be able to hear what your team mate is saying, that means not having a loud bang from the muzzle right next to your ear! If you have ever been in a room with people shooting next to your ear you will know what I mean. Benefits of suppressors include:

1. Suppressor for sound, making it harder to find you at distance.
2. Flash suppression, as the enemy will shoot at your flash signature.
3. To improve your hearing for communication, to hear approach enemy, etc.
4. Better for room clearing because the sound of gunfire in a room is extremely loud and disorientating. It is almost as bad a flash bang in a room without the shock wave and flash of a flash bang, but it's *very loud*

Beware they don't take well to large volumes of rounds being shot as they tend to overheat and even melt, so consider the type of operation and potential type of contact or engagements you might have with the enemy. The images below show a suppressor and another one cut in half exposing the intricate "baffle" designs for suppressing noise:

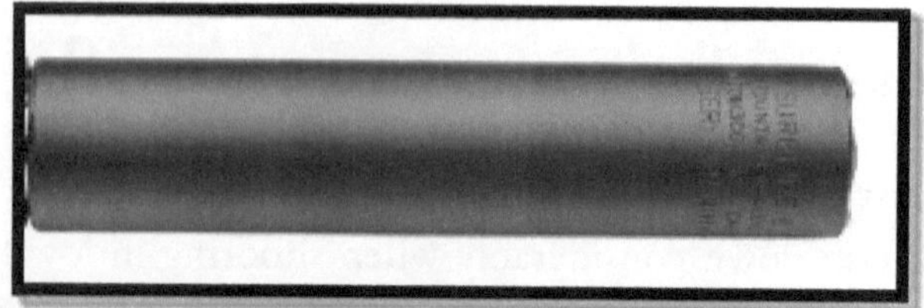

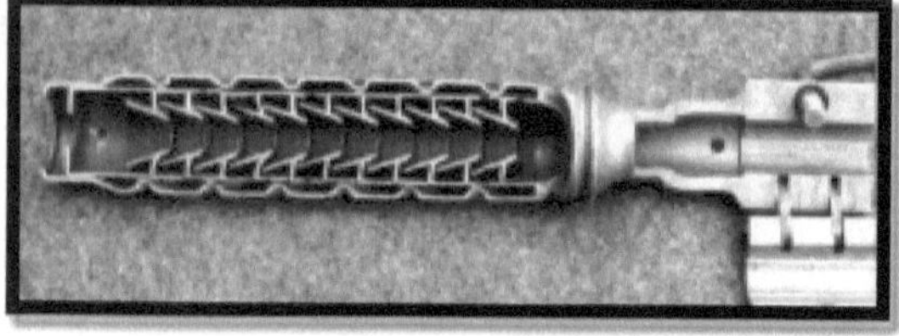

Chest webbing

When using a rifle for PSD (close protection), or any combat purposes, the magazines will be carried in chest webbing, leg rig or some sort of chest pouch but can also be carried in a small backpack (especially when working on PSD operations). Carrying extra magazines can be done in any configurations that suit the individual. Focus on using a configuration and layout familiar to you from your training, as that layout will be subconsciously efficient, which means grabbing a magazine in a real combat situation will feel second nature. This will take extensive training to take it to a subconscious level of performance needed to function in real combat.

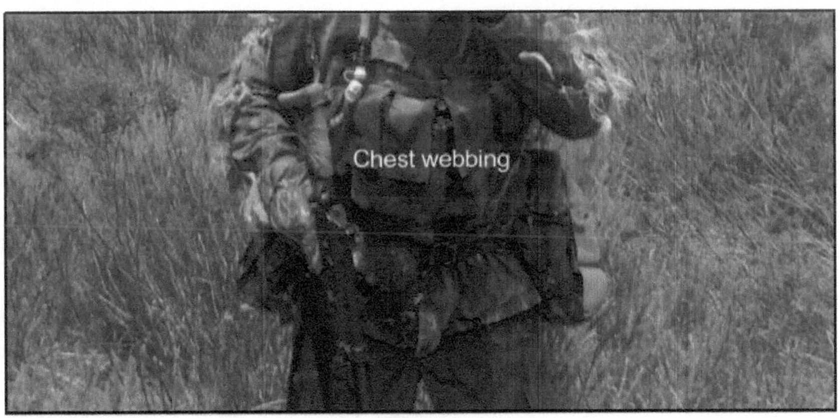

Thermal vision

The purpose for this would be identifying (ID) an attacker or enemy in the dark. Such an individual stands out quite clearly at ranges from 100-300 meters depending on the quality of and magnification of the thermal scope. Thermal will give you a distinct advantage over an enemy lacking such capability although thermal scopes are very expensive. These devices are used for hog hunting and are proven very capable of engaging 2 or 3 targets in succession if the open ground is available. I haven't personally tested any of the thermal scopes in the pictures yet so I can't give you my opinion on any specific brands but *I would go for a military specification scope* to be safe, as these should be robust and reliable.

Thermal scope

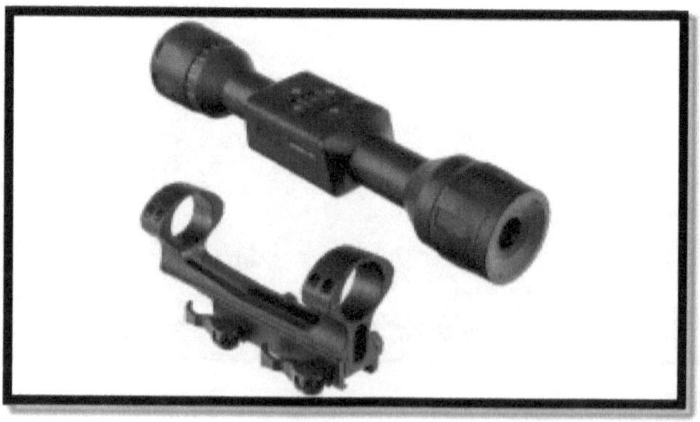

Thermal scope

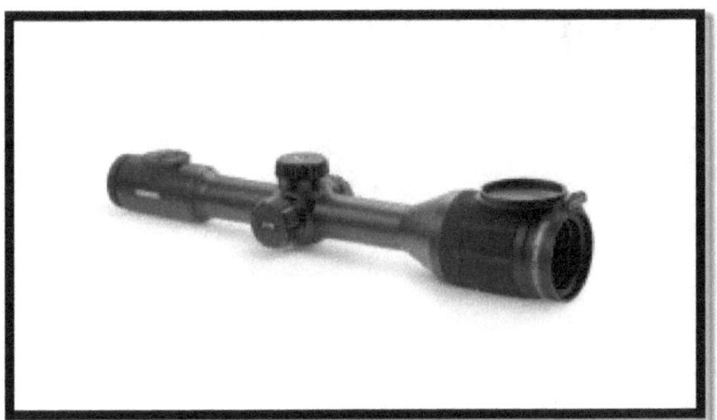

Weapon Carry Techniques

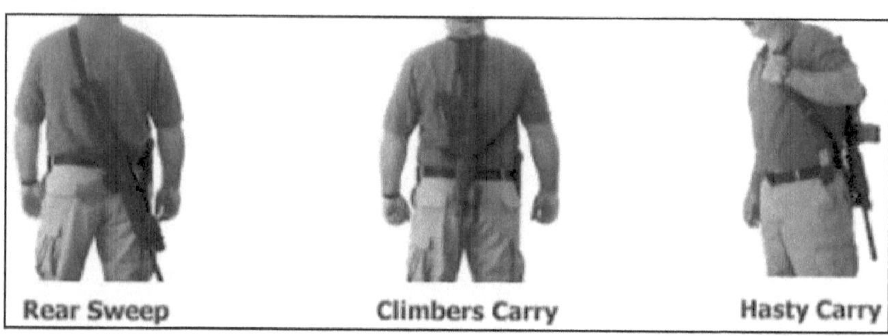

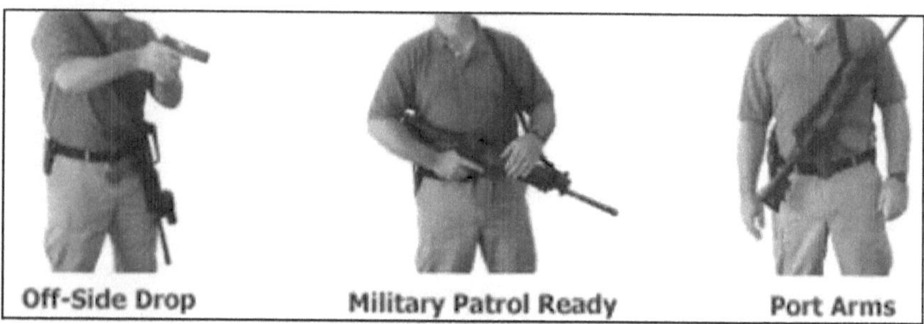

Best carry position for the combat rifle when in small teams is high port (barrel facing sky wards) as this negates most accidents, and if an accidental discharge happens then the round won't possibly ricochet off the ground into someone's legs. If you are operating on your own then it doesn't matter as it's only the enemy that you have to worry about.

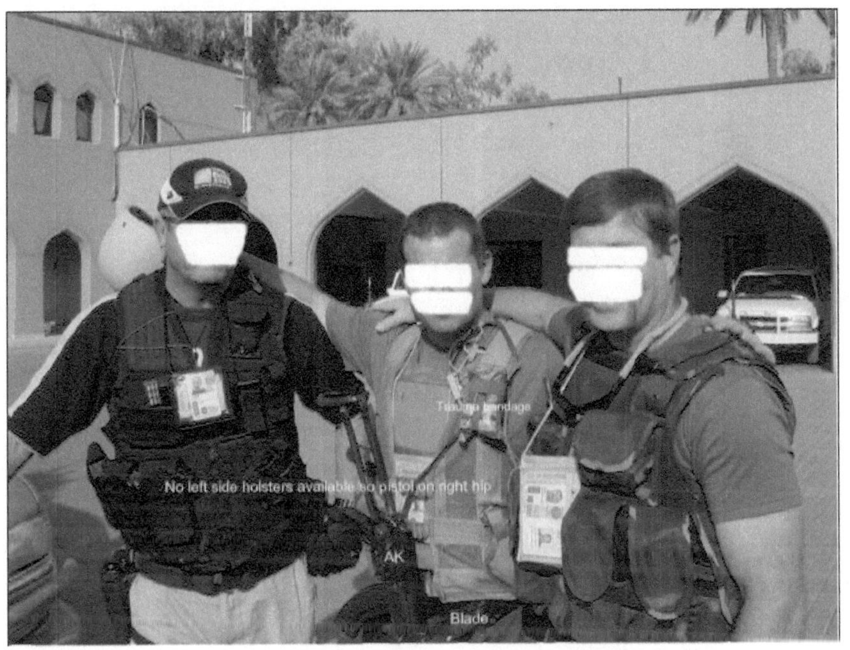
Trauma bandage
No left side holsters available so pistol on right hip
AK
Blade

Carry in a war zone (SHTF)

Best configuration practice for a war zone

- The best weapons carry configuration is to *have as many of your weapons available to both hands as possible.* This is due to the potential for injury to your hands from a ballistic point of view as well as mechanical injury due to cuts, or abrasions from e.g., putting your hands down on the ground in a combat environment. You just have to do the most rudimentary research to find out how easy and fast you can get shot in the hand and you will have insight into why you have a weapon available to both hands. This applies to ballistic weapons and blades as combat can go from far to close range quickly.

- Your rifle, which is your primary weapon, is controlled by your dominant hand (right hand for most people). Chest webbing with 6 magazines carrying 30 rounds per magazine is a minimum, and have 3 magazines for the pistol (1 in the pistol and two spare). One inserted pistol magazine and 4 spare is also doable and can normally fit on the belt if you are not carrying too much other equipment. How much you carry depends on how far you are from resupply and what your function is at that point in time.

- Your pistol is placed on the weak hand side (left hand for most people) so that you can access it with your weak hand if your dominant hand is injured or busy with your rifle. This might not seem important, but in reality, the chances of being shot in your strong/dominant hand that is holding a weapon is greater than you think. The smaller the target area you present, the more likely you will be shot in the hand as your enemy focuses on what they can see and if they can only see your head and hand then this is what they will shoot at. If you were standing up then they have the whole body to shoot at and therefore it's less likely that you will be shot in the hand. Many people that were in both modern and pre 1900 century wars, where rifles (muskets or modern rifles) were used, have been wounded in the hand, because of this body part exposure issue.

- Your knife (small fighting knife, 5-7 inches of blade roughly speaking) can be placed on your belt in such a way that it is accessible by both your left and right hand. Placing it across your body level on your belt does this. At this level it is also out of direct line of sight of the enemy, which is important in combat as you don't want to give the enemy an advantage in any way. A fighting knife should be at least 8-12 inches long and a survival knife can be 3-4 inches as seen in most survival programs. Even though it's highly unlikely that you would be using a blade in a combat, it's likely that you want to have it as a backup for close in fighting or for weapon retention.

Mode (carrying condition) for your rifle

<u>Condition 1</u>: Cocked, loaded, safety on (this is how most are carried in hostile areas). To get your rifle into action you take your safety off and aim. This is a fast way to engage targets, the downside is if the safety comes off in noncombative circumstances you might have an accidental discharge with dire consequences. It's not that hard to bump the safety off when you have chest webbing and metal clips and all sorts of places that the safety could hook onto and disengage.

<u>Condition 2</u>: Cocked and unloaded (full magazine, no round in chamber) with safety off. This works well for the AK derivative rifles. To get your rifle into action you rack the cocking handle, without a magazine in, and then put the full magazine in, carried in this condition to allow more safety but to allow the weapon to be loaded quickly with less effort and no safety so it's very fast.

<u>Condition 3</u>: Un–cocked and unloaded, no round in the chamber, magazine in (not recommended). To get your rifle into action you take your safety off and rack the cocking handle. This will be ok in an environment where you are not expecting a contact. This condition will sometimes be used by a person in charge of a group of mostly untrained combatants or low level security or military units.

Always consider the direction a bullet will travel if you fall and the barrel might become filled with mud or sand and cause a major risk to you and surrounding operators if it blows up. This has actually happened to a friend who is a SF operator; he got shot in the calf by a fellow operator by accident when they were doing some house penetration drills.

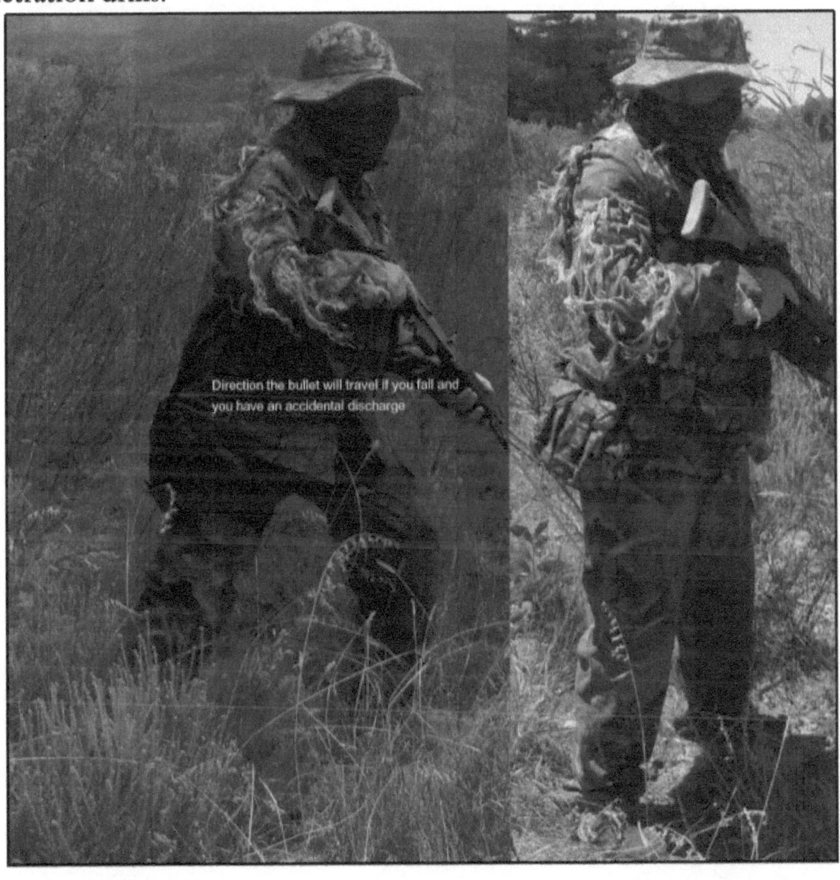

Combat Load Out Options

Pure combat load out

This section describes how to master combat with your well-placed load out equipment.

Using the configuration (as shown below) for combat, whether military, PSD or civil unrest SHTF, gives you the ability to hold the rifle in a position to fire without dropping it. It also means you have the pistol to cover another angle if needed. The blade positioning allows you to access it with both hands for use, to be used in primary weapon retention if needed. You will notice the load out is not complicated, just very efficient for medium and close-range combat. I have taught this to my students that make it to a higher level of combat proficiency for about 16-17 years. It makes common sense to have your equipment ready to both hands as it's both *expedient and efficient*. Be very careful and *put the blade back slowly* as you don't want to stab yourself in the groin, where the femoral artery is.

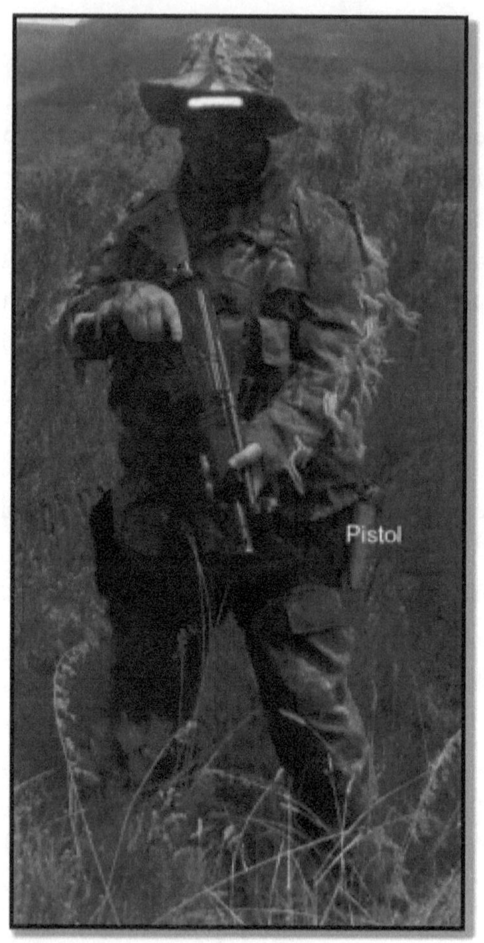
Pistol

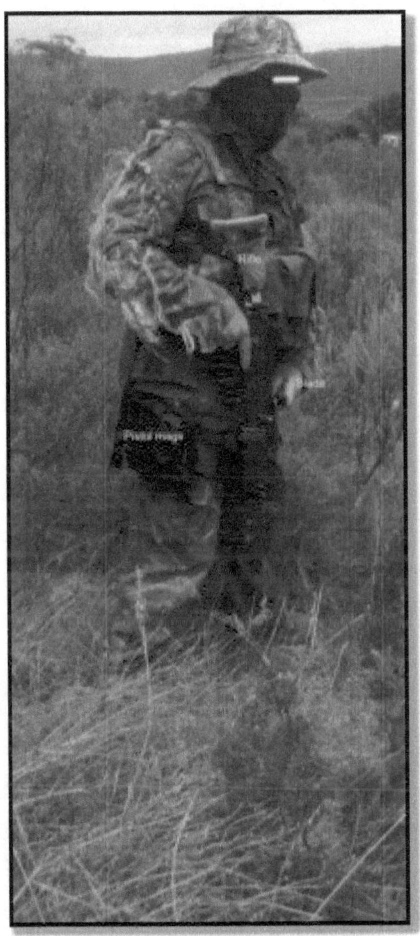

For the pistol, you need to practice taking the safety off with your weak hand or swap to a gun without a manual safety e.g., Glock). Training quite extensively to make this configuration work, it isn't easy and needs a lot of work. Don't look at your equipment when accessing it – try as much as possible to feel where the equipment is. This will give you the confidence and quick access you will need in a combat environment where efficiency is important. Efficiency means speed and accuracy with least effort; this will also include movement and all other aspects of combat efficiency.

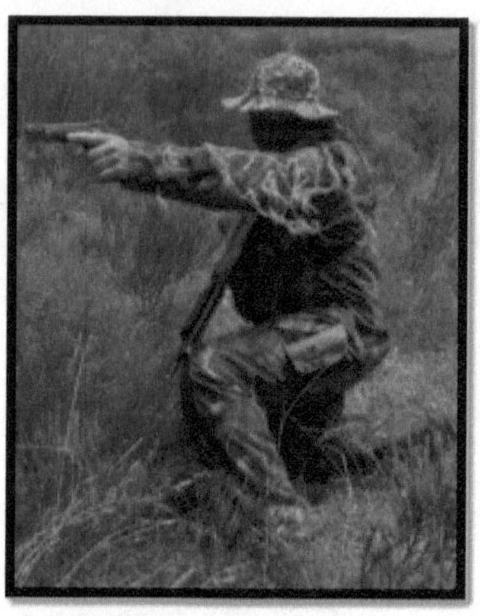

Having your blade **high on your webbing** puts it **in front of an opponent's eyes** ready for them to grab. The knife grip shown below is called "forward" grip, which can easily be changed into "reverse" grip. Forward grip will give you more range but reverse grip is normally considered a stronger grip. Reverse grip lends itself to strong downward stabbing, but forward grip can give you subtle arm cutting and quick thrusting options. Always choose the longest practical blade for combat as it gives you reach, and in blade on blade or even retention for your handgun and rifle it will be easier for you when you have more reach.

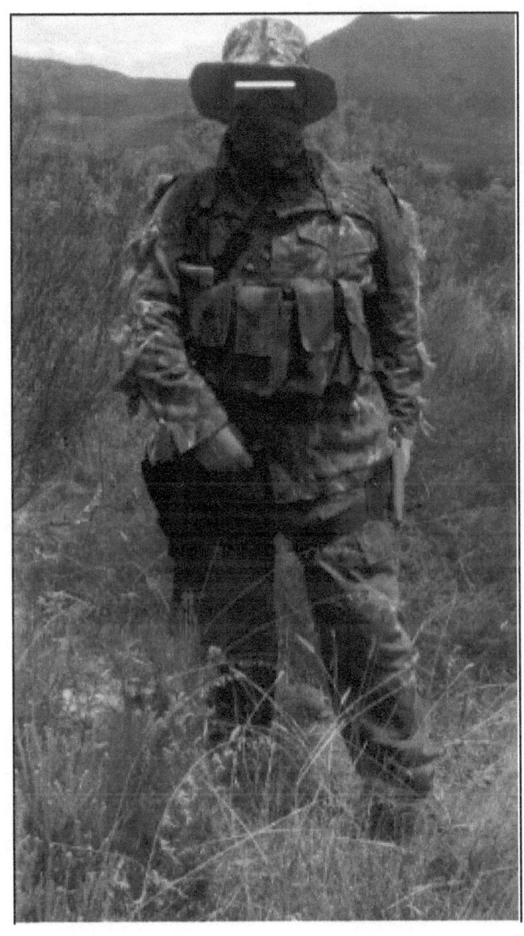

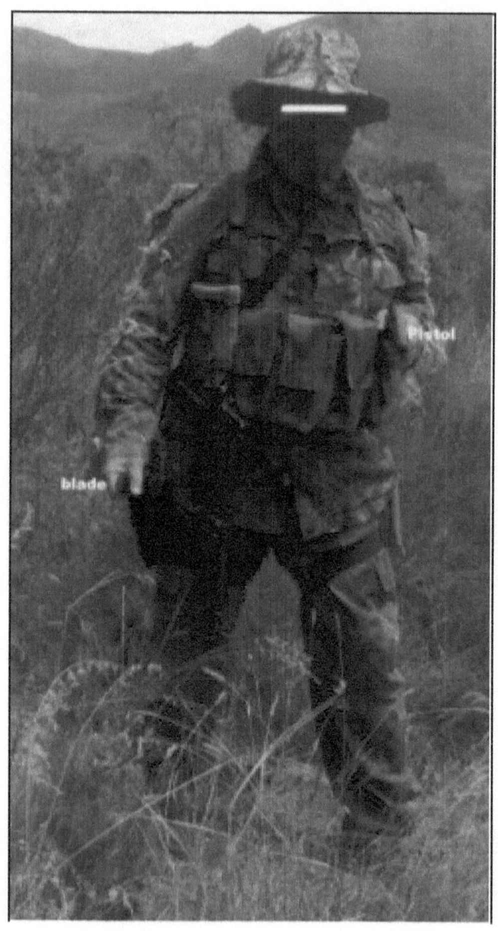

The pictures below show changing the blade from forward grip to reverse grip. This combination gives you the best presentation (accessing ability) to use handgun and then your blade as a pistol retention implement; this is the reason for this combination and configuration. Having your equipment close at hand and quickly accessible is one of the foundations of real combat efficiency and helps or goes a long way to making you fast and efficient.

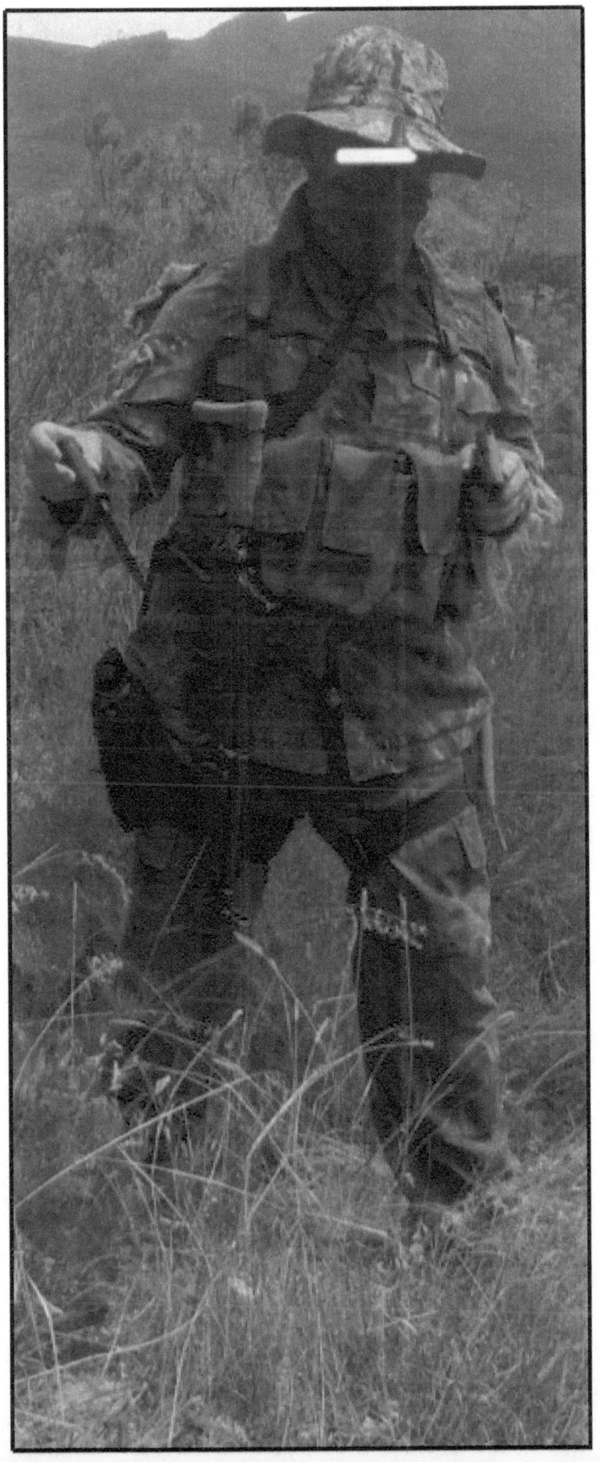

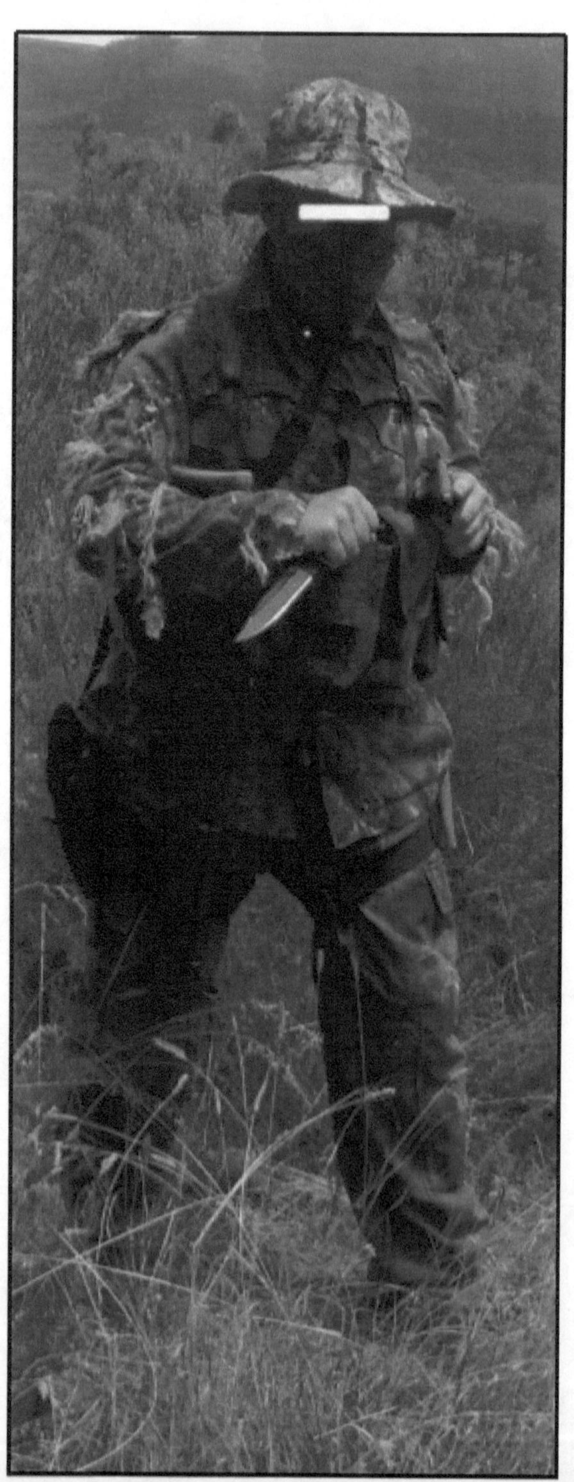

In the pictures below, we see the blade in reverse grip in weak hand while the strong hand is on the rifle which can still be held in that hand while using the blade, ready for engaging targets by bringing the rifle up, as the hand is still on the pistol grip and in an appropriate position. Your blade should be primarily used for rifle retention as your rifle is far more lethal in combat than the pistol or blade. You can shoot out ammunition at an alarming rate in combat so make sure you have enough ammunition if you are expecting combat. The blade is primarily used for survival and weapon retention and should be consider only when absolutely necessary and last resort – it's not even a secondary weapon but more for use if are down to nothing. That doesn't mean you should ignore training with it, you should know the basic use of the blade and its capabilities.

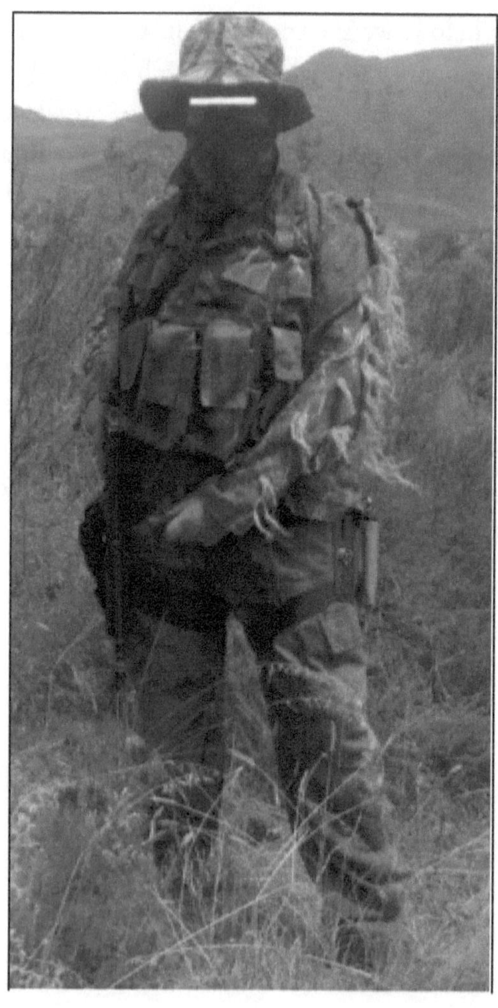

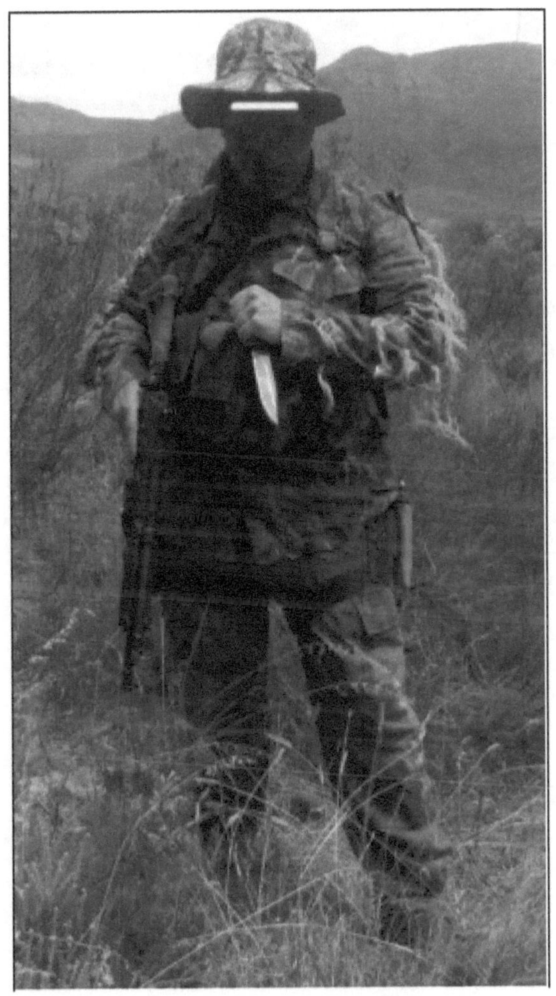

Equipment load out for patrolling and reconnaissance

As shown in the pictures below, essential equipment will include:

- Extra magazines
- Shorter rifle magazines
- Compass and radio
- Food, water (colloquially often called "H2O"), suitable head gear
- Suitable camouflage clothing and accessories
- Survival gear e.g., fire starting equipment and water filtration options
- Medical equipment.

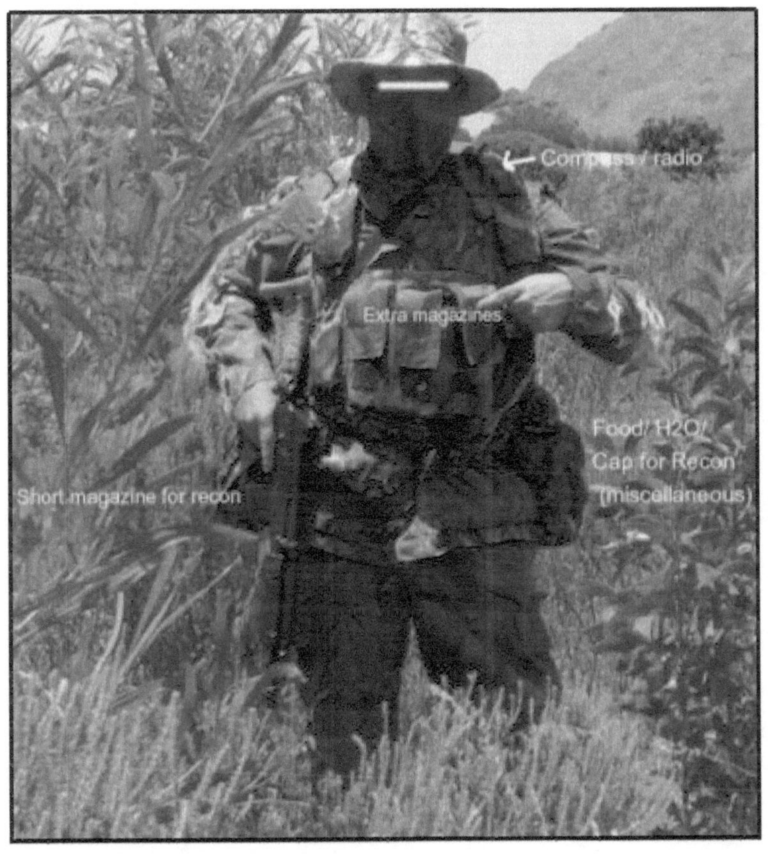

Compass / radio
Extra magazines
Food/ H2O/
Cap for Recon
(miscellaneous)
Short magazine for recon

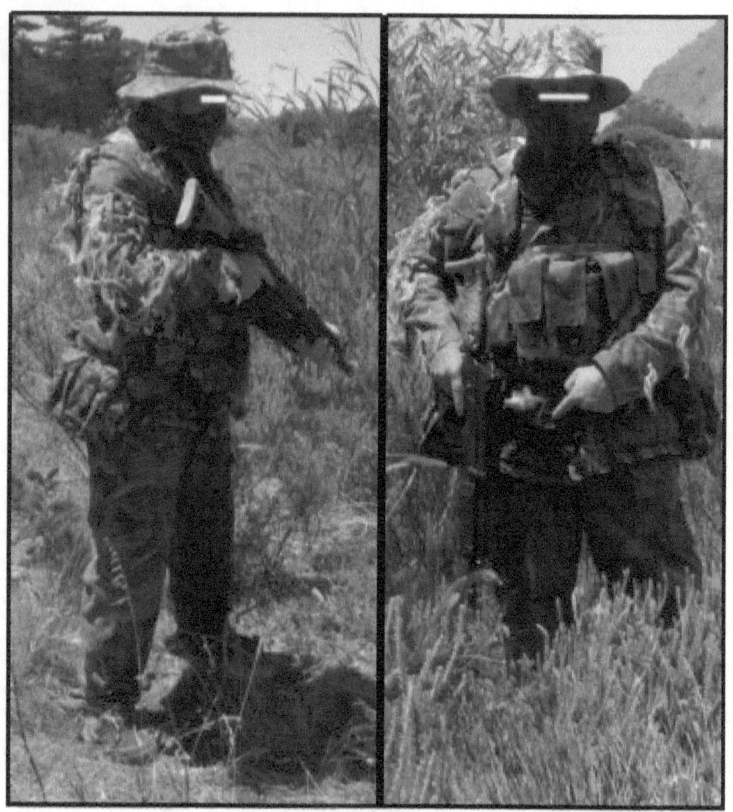

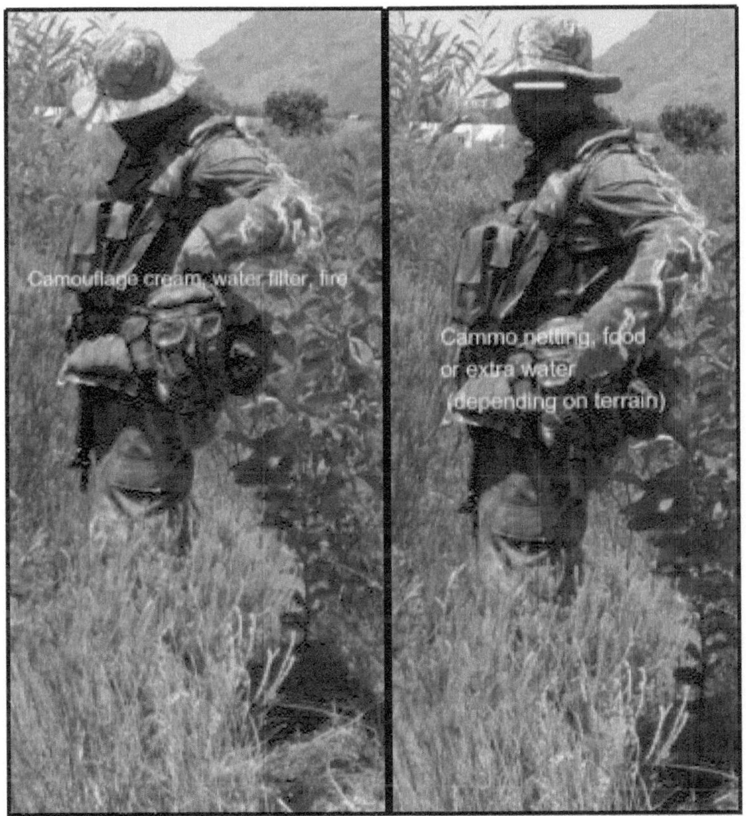
Camouflage cream, water filter, fire
Cammo netting, food
or extra water
(depending on terrain)

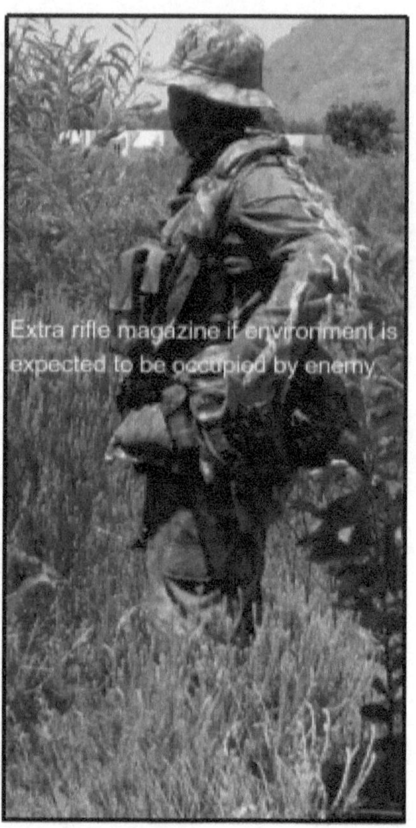
Extra rifle magazine if environment is
expected to be occupied by enemy.

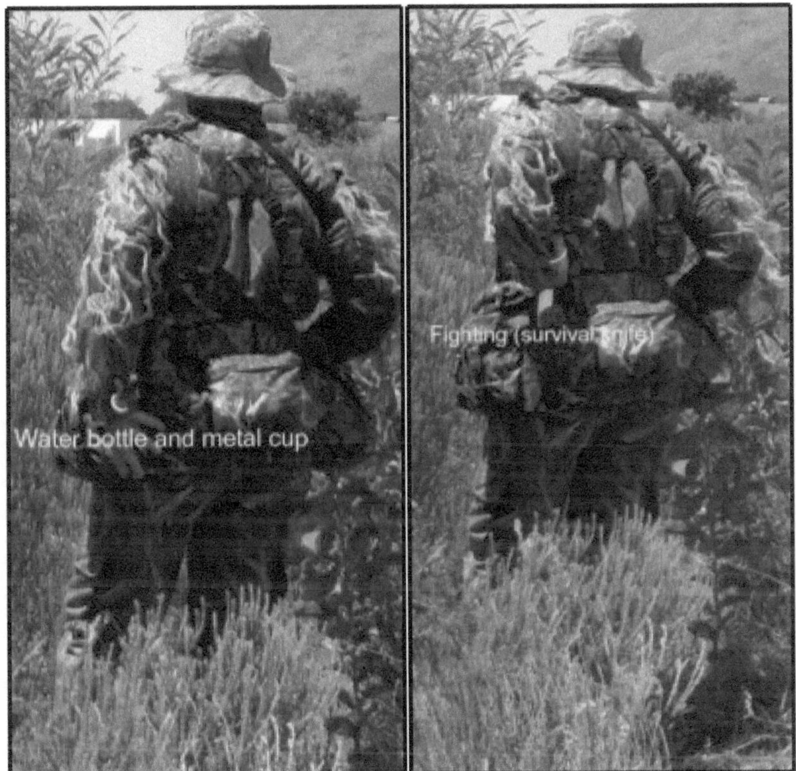
Fighting (survival knife)
Water bottle and metal cup

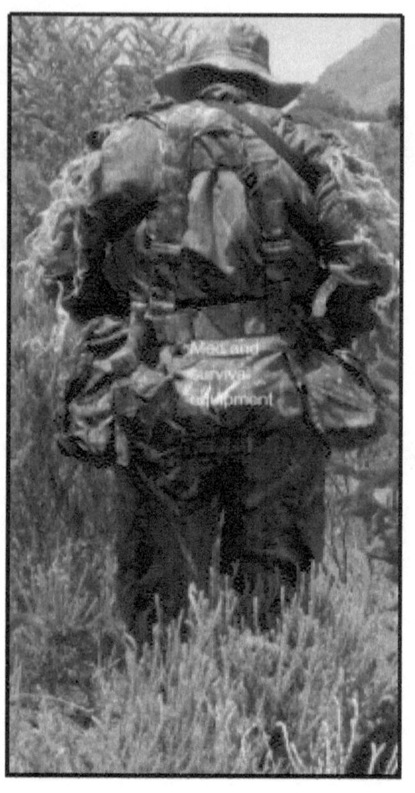

Load out for extended patrolling

In addition to the load out above, use a backpack, carry what you can handle comfortably, don't overload the backpack as fatigue will cause you to become slack and lose focus.

This larger backpack will carry the other items too large or heavy for recon/patrolling.

The following is an example of loud out but is not by any means the only equipment you could carry or use in a combat scenario. The equipment load out could also be affected by who is supplying you and your objectives. The secret is to only carry what is absolutely necessary. This is dictated by your objectives and goals:

1. Sleeping bag, plus a shelter sheet to cover you from rain and sun, and a ground sheet will keep you from losing heat to the ground. This set up must be well thought out and comprehensive to allow a good sleep so you don't fatigue and make mistakes while on operation.

2. Extra food (depending on type and duration of operation). This will be your long-term food which should not be sweats and sugary stuff but more protein, fats and vitamin and minerals you get from dried fruit and nuts for example. A good protein source would be dried meat (beef jerky or pemmican) and fats could be from meat which is good for you if you don't get it from cows that were injected with hormones and antibiotics. Grass-fed free-range cows that were healthy and were not injected with steroids, antibiotics and hormones are your best choice.

3. Comprehensive medical (this might not be as relevant if only on a purely reconnaissance mission) especially for long range reconnaissance.

4. Optional gas stove. Doesn't give off smoke, gives off very little

smell (quick and easy boiling of water, and for food). I would consider this a luxury item unless reconnaissance is your goal where fire is impossible. This does add to your bulk and size of the of the overall pack.

5. Extra water (in bladder) or spare 1 liter bottle (depending on type of operation). This is one of the essential items of your kit, so having the ability to expand your water by using extra soft bags that can fold up in your kit and can be used when needed is essential to long term water storage.

6. Spotter scope (depending on type of operation). Allows you to observe the enemy, look for a path ahead in situations where the terrain allows, identify game for hunting, and observe your team mates in their area of operations e.g., close reconnaissance, if terrain allows for this (such as from a hill that overlooks the area where the enemy are located).

7. Extra ammo (depending on type of operation). This is another essential item that once you run out of it's going to be a bad day if the enemy are intent on dispatching you to the happy hunting ground. The only way to have large amounts available to you is to have caches in your area of operations (AO). The heavier your pack the harder you work but if you hit a contact then it's worth it but on the flip side you are also going to be fatigued more easily.

8. Large plastic bag (heavy duty plastic) can be used for river crossings or cache (not the same as a dry bag). ***Dry bag*** is even better as this keeps all essential items dry and can serve as a large water carrier in emergency, helps your backpack to float when doing river crossings. Most camping shops will sell a heavy duty plastic bag for putting equipment in and or as an emergency sleeping bag.

9. Inside main compartment ***dry bag*** for emergency clothes, ammunition (hunting or combat). The bag can be

5–15-liters. This also helps keep everything together for compression, this is where your dry socks would be kept and T-shirt in case of getting soaked in rain in very cold climate.

10. Spare compass (back up). This is also used to verify that your other compass in your combat webbing works correctly. You might have a watch with a compass function so you can use that to ensure that the main compass is working correctly. It's one of the essentials if you are in a combat environment that requires you to be at a certain place in a certain time. If combined with a good quality GPS and a map, you should not have much chance of getting lost unless you are totally inexperienced or incompetent at land navigation.

11. Pad and pencil can be for making maps of the area (AO), writing notes to team mates that might be in a distant OP/LP e.g., notes for the radio operator to send to HQ, writing notes on edible plants in area, recording enemy disposition etc. Try to get waterproof paper.

12. Depending on operational requirements, a map of AO can give you distances from your OP (observation points) to the target. This is essential when engaging the enemy at distance with your precision rifle. I wouldn't put cache sites on the map unless you have a way of disguising it (in the event you lose the map to the enemy) but this is another aspect to consider. A map also helps to locate and plan operations e.g., cache sites.

13. Camouflage cream. This is only applicable for situations where concealment is your goal therefore it's more for military situations and SHTF scenarios. This will be relevant in a combat patrolling scenario or reconnaissance role. Basically any situation where stealth and camouflage is relevant.

14. Water purification is in the belt webbing, if only the main bag

is carried then they will be in main bag. This also includes tourniquet and signal mirror and or radio that would normally be in belt webbing.

15. Specialized equipment could be night vision, thermal imaging, laser designator (military), range finder, specialized surveillance equipment such as drones etc. You won't be able to put all these in your bag; one or two are possible such as Night Vision and range finder is possible.

Example showing entering LP/OP (listening post /observation post). This is normally a place where you rest up for a short period of time or where you observe a target area. It can also be a place to do reconnaissance on an enemy base:

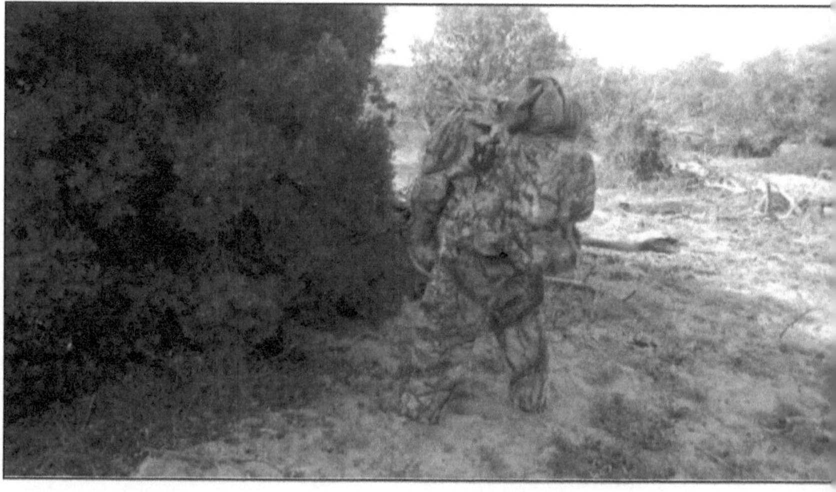

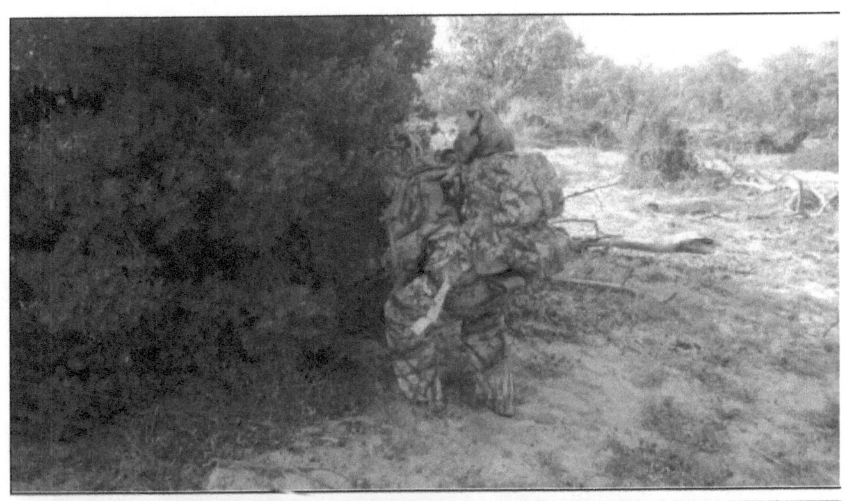

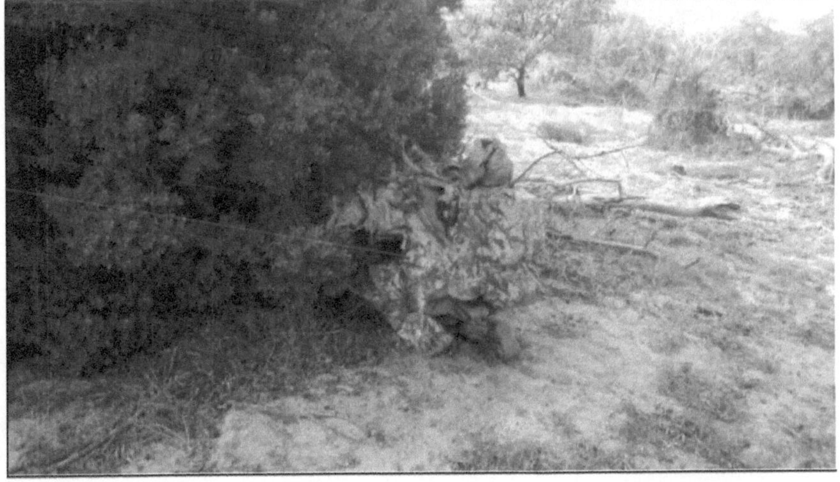

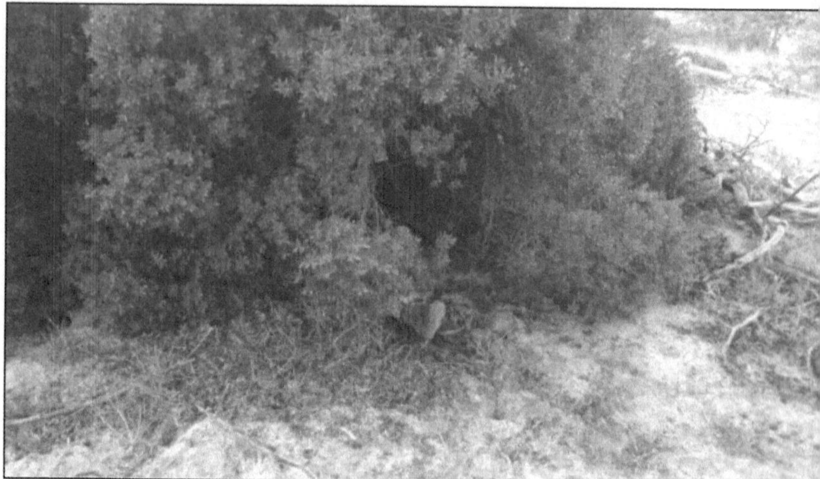

Once in your LP/OP, you should be substantially hidden. This does not mean that you haven't left sign outside the (LUP) lay-up place. And your tracks will be left along the path you walked, even when taking great pains to leave very little "sign" (using anti tracking techniques or wiping sign with very light brush strokes).

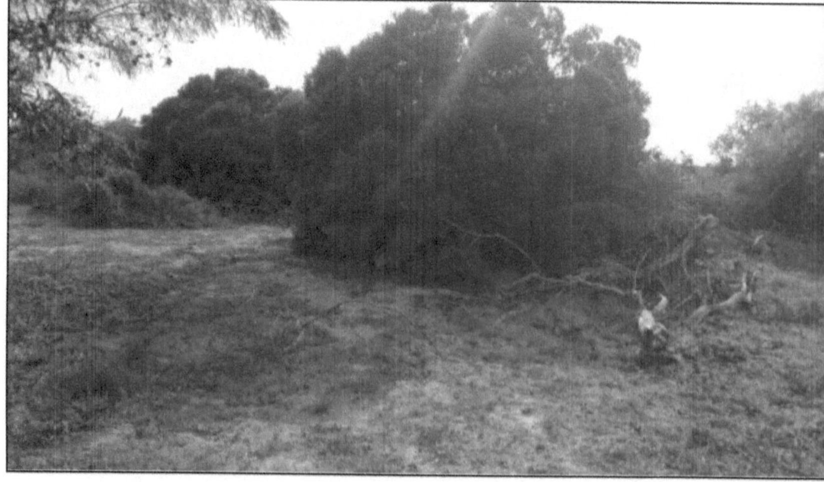

Camouflage for Dry Terrain

Example A

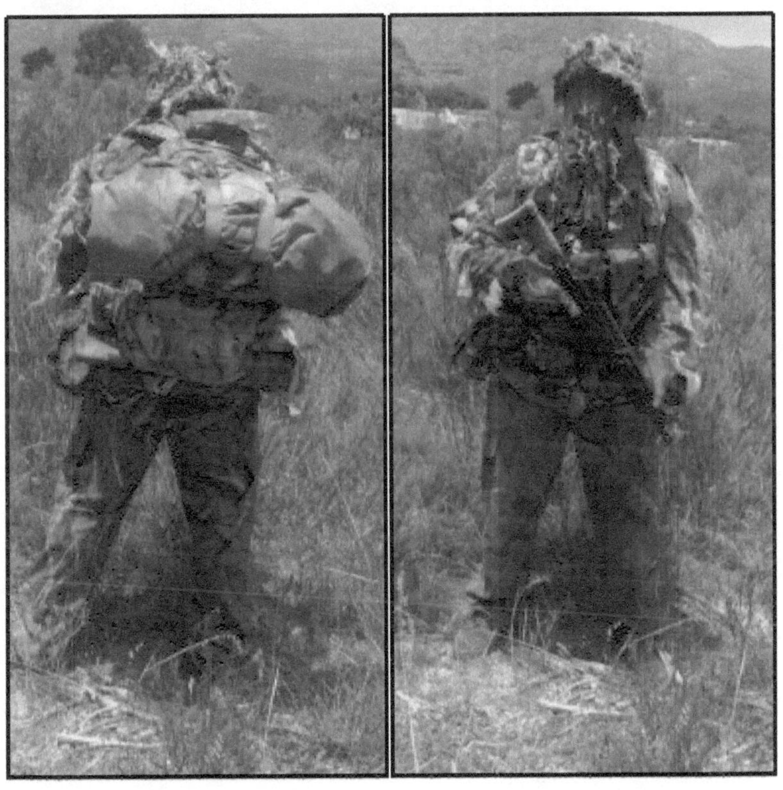

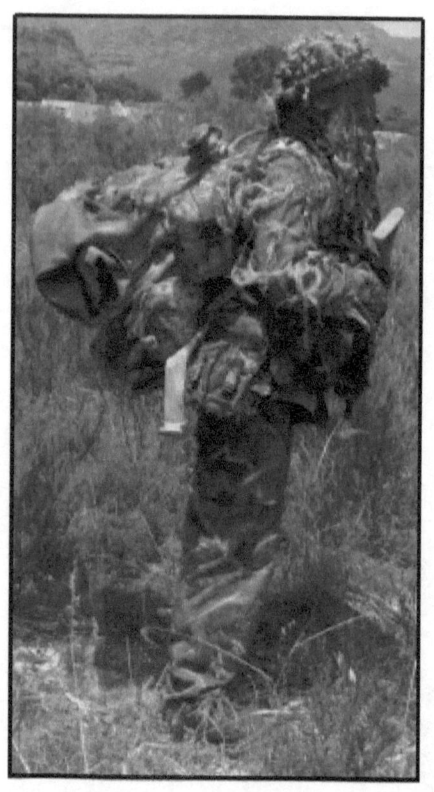

Example B

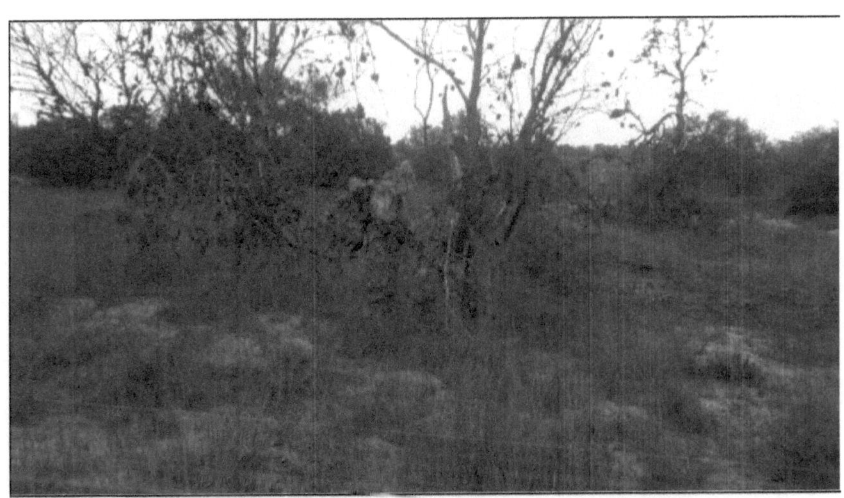

Blend your camouflage so that it flows as this makes it more effective:

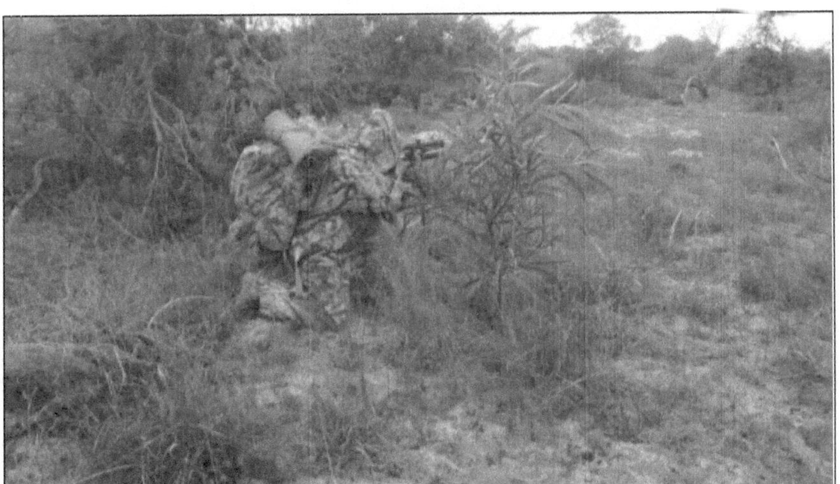

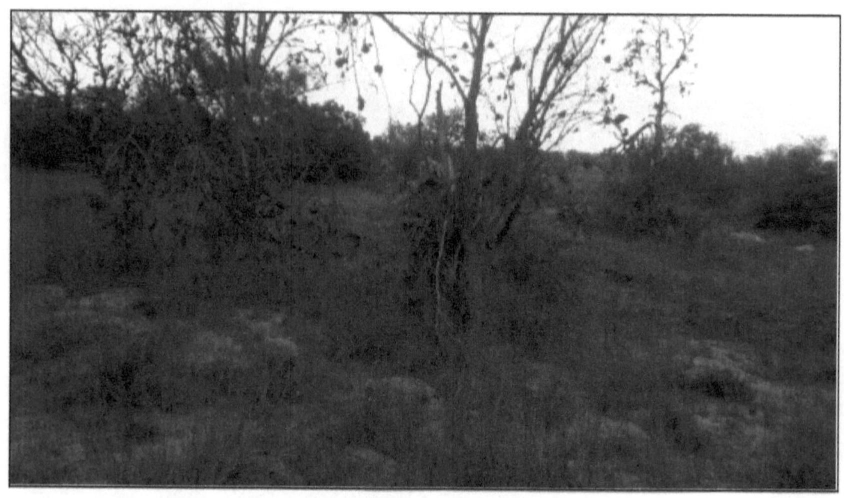

Below is an enlargement of the camouflaged individual:

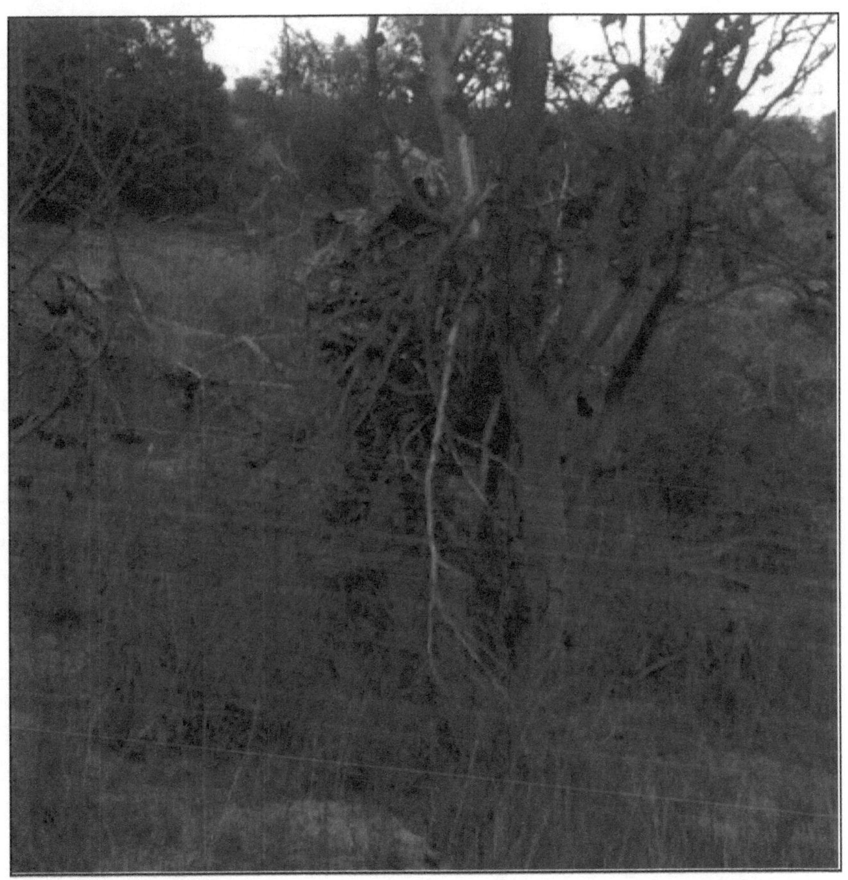

Camouflage for Green Terrain

Here the vegetation is mostly olive green and therefore camouflage will be mostly olive green:

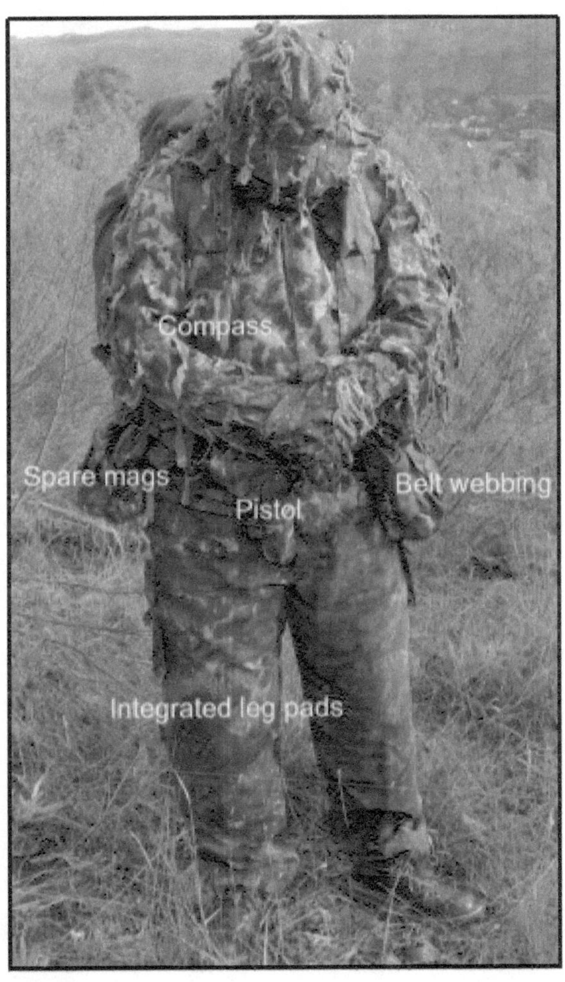
Compass
Spare mags
Pistol
Belt webbing
Integrated leg pads

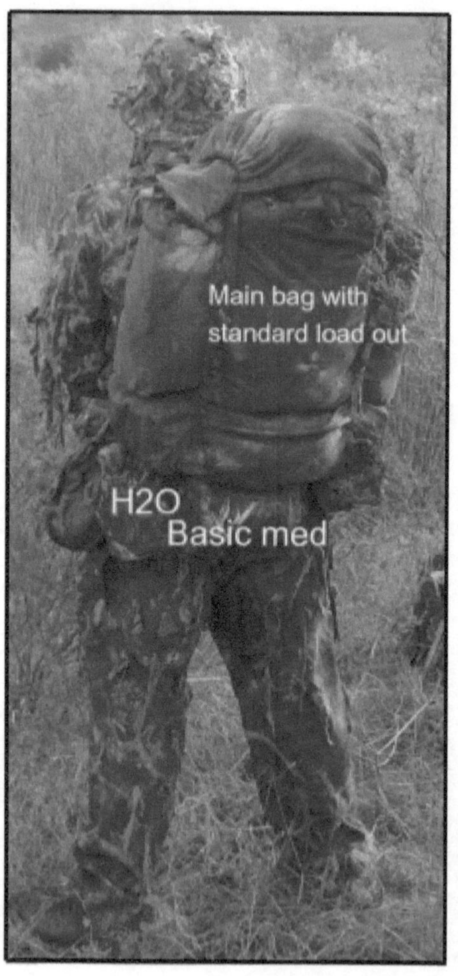
Main bag with
standard load out
H2O
Basic med

Carry for Reconnaissance, Patrolling and Combat

Applications include **trench warfare / house clearing, close range** within walking distance of your FOB (forward operating base).Trenches are used in limited situation all over the world still today and is therefore relevant

Further enhancements to your reconnaissance load out can be made by adding a backpack like the "Camelback" brand because the backpack has a water bladder e.g., for an extra 3 liters. This would allow patrolling in a desert type environment where you will be close to your observation post or base (OP/LP). You can also use this configuration for patrolling close to your FOB. You could also use a small 15-20 liter backpack to allow a bit more equipment if traveling further, as reconnaissance and observation might demand the use of scopes or binoculars or even night vision and or thermal imager.

This load out is for civilian use, the only difference is if you were a **military unit**, you might add grenades to the load out and maybe encrypted communications. You might want to have a fighting knife at the front and a survival knife on the belt webbing at back as indicated. Keep the equipment as light as possible; you don't want to run with excessive weight on your body in the heat. Exhaustion is a morale sapper and is debilitating to anyone who is not super fit.

Don't carry any items that are not *absolutely necessary*, because <u>extra weight</u> *slows you down* and makes you tired, when you are *tired you are more likely to make mistakes*, less likely to tread lightly and more likely to stumble onto the enemy. This can be a deadly encounter if they notice you first, so carry light and stay alert.

- Try to keep it simple and light. **Once you know your specific objectives** for the patrol or reconnaissance or ambush role then you will have a clearer understanding of what you want to take.

- ○ E.g., if I were to do a reconnaissance function then I would also have a thermal monocular for observation of the target and maybe an NV (night vision) monocular.
- ○ If it were more of a mission based on locating an objective (target) I would carry extra navigation equipment to make sure I could pass on the correct information to HQ (headquarters). This would then also include encrypted radios for communication.

- Only carry what you ***absolutely** need, not what **you think** you need or what you hope you will need.* You might think you need 3-4 days' worth of food but water is more important as you can go without food for 2-3 weeks in an emergency but only 3-4 days without water. Bushmen of the Kalahari drink maybe 500 ml in a day and live in one of the hottest climates (desert) on the planet. This is because of conditioning and ***should not be attempted by you*** without **prior conditioning training**.
- **Make sure everything works**, this includes equipment in the webbing and the webbing itself, radios with correct channels, adequate water, ammo, maps and compass, camouflage cream for face, survival items like fire making matches or fire steel, spare water bag to increase water carrying capacity for dry areas where water is scarce etc.
- If it's for recon purpose that you are patrolling then tape everything so it ***can't make a noise. Jump up and down to test this as someone helps you to listen for noise.***

Some major items to consider:

1. Water bottle and canteen cup (stainless steel metal). This is also a good place to store chemicals for water purifying if you

don't want to use a fire to boil it. A fire might be **too overt** – if you are in a combat environment, *fire* can be seen and **smelt over great distances**. Time might be of the essence as you might be in an E&E (escape and evade) situation, so having a chemical option is always good.

2. Survival / fighting knife (this configuration doesn't lend itself to combat but more general operations). A survival knife can be short and light (full tang), a fighting knife should be long and very sharp, at minimum 6 inches. A survival blade can be short, preferably full tang and a few mm thick for stoutness. It can be light and small like a Mora.

3. Veil/scarf for head and face (good for LP/OP) helps to disrupt the shape of the head and can be used to observe the enemy as it is easy to see through. It does help in the cold as a lot of heat is lost through the head and neck area. It can also be suspended in front of your hide to allow you to see through while watching a target. In an emergency if you can tie it tight then you might be able to make an improvised tourniquet.

4. Basic medical and or survival items at back (you can either put a tourniquet on the webbing in one of small poaches at front high or on outside at the top). If possible, add a pouch with *quick clot* at the front next to the *tourniquet* (quick clot burns when you apply it to a wound so just get ready for that mentally). You only need the very basics such as electrolytes for heat exhaustion, something for diarrhea, pain killers, and any personal meds you prefer/require.

5. Side pockets are for food and extra water container (plastic fold up type container) specifically for dry areas. Use very basic high energy foods. This could mean anything that doesn't "go off" (spoil) in hot environments but gives you a lot of energy for the size and weight of the food. Preferably

not too many sweet or sugary items, rather oil or fat and protein (these don't cause you to have an increased insulin surge). Old style biltong/beef jerky is one of the best for energy and health reasons, and nuts and raisins (assuming no nut allergies).

6. Fire making device in small pouch on sides. Fires won't be used on recon but maybe if away from the objective and you need heat at night if cold or need to cook or boil water. Hot tea or coffee goes a long way to picking your mood up when you are freezing. Have at least **3 ways of making fire** e.g. matches, lighter and fire steel.

7. Camouflage creams. These are only used when on combat patrol, or when in close recon. Any time you feel extra camouflage is needed. That's why it is in the side small pouch where they can be easily accessed and applied to maintain the effect. This will also be addressed by your team mates if and when they notice your camouflage degrading.

8. Place for 4 extra magazines in belt webbing so your total magazines with chest webbing is 10 and with two (double magazine taped together) on the rifle that makes 12 total. With each magazine being 30 rounds, 12 x 30 = 360 rounds. This will make a good combat load for assault or ambush or general patrolling if you are not too far from the base (FOB), and would be even more important if you are a **small team** like a 2-4 man team.

9. Binocular in the front small pouch. Always use the best quality binocular and even better would be a **high quality monocular (smaller and lighter)**. The clearer you can see the better you can identify potential problems. The better you can plan and decide whether to either engage the enemy or evade them. Identifying weapon systems and other equipment of the enemy will help you greatly.

10. Compass/GPS in top small pouch. It's going to be important to know where you are especially if you are reporting on enemy movements. GPS gives a nice accurate position but only works if it can access the satellites e.g., a forest makes it difficult.

11. For your basic survival items take a look at the basics of what Bushmen carry: knife, fire making equipment, maybe small axe or throwing stick, bow and maybe ostrich egg shell for water. We would use a rifle as a primary and stainless steel water bottle, otherwise it's not very different from what they carry.

Example of basic equipment layout for SHTF, patrolling or reconnaissance

In this section, we see a basic equipment load out applying the above principles. This load out allows you to expand your magazine count to 10 if needed or you can keep it at 6 in chest and 1 or 2 on the weapon system. You also have the option of dropping your main bag to do a recon, or in the event of a contact and you need to make a tactical withdrawal. This also allows you to carry either 1 litre of water or up to 5 or 6 litres depending on the terrain. This load out is adaptable for reconnaissance, combat or patrolling.

Here's an improvised shelter connected to your bag using a "Bivy" (bivouac) sheet:

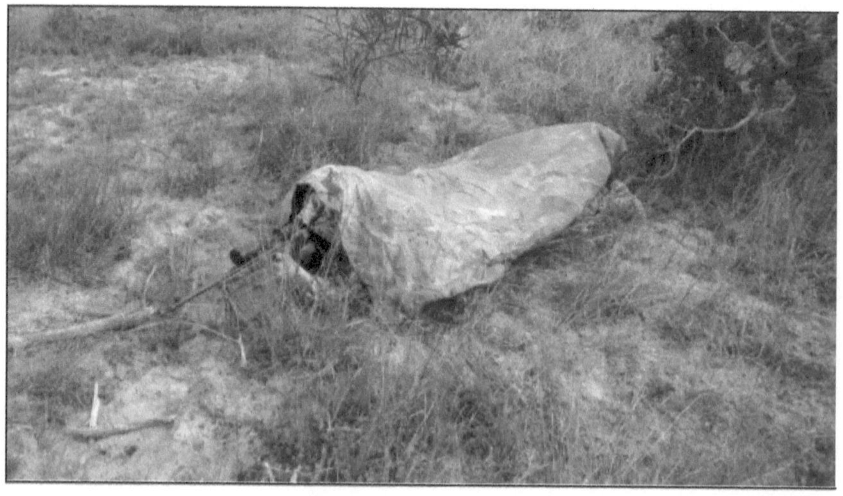

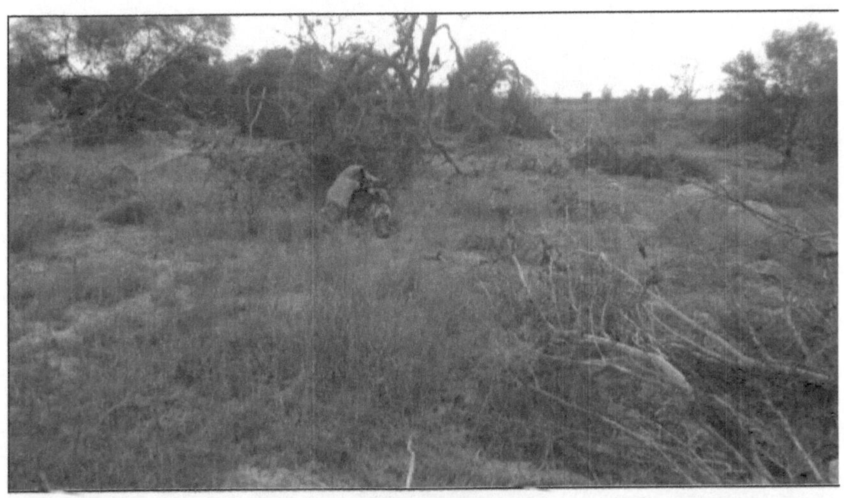

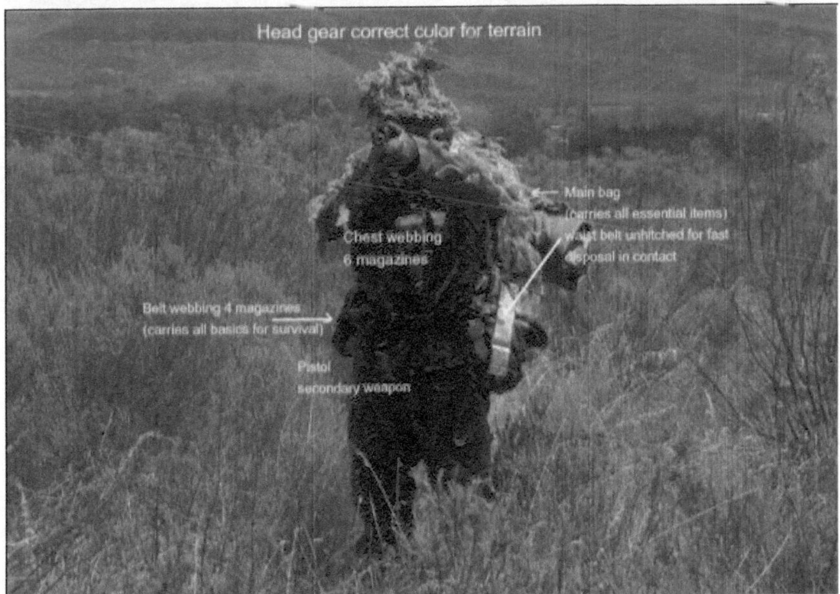

When using the position shown below, you would have more than likely **dropped** your **main bag** (30-40kg) to allow easier movement. Of course, your shins are exposed to enemy fire even in this scenario, but getting shot in the shin is not nearly as bad as being shot in the femoral artery:

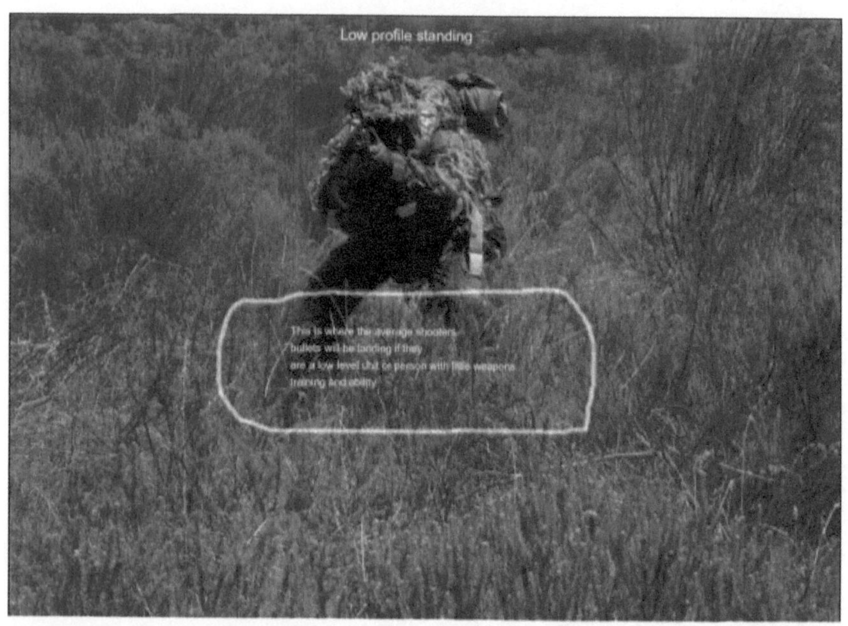
Low profile standing
This is where the average shooters
bullets will be landing if they
are a low level unit or person with little weapons
training and ability

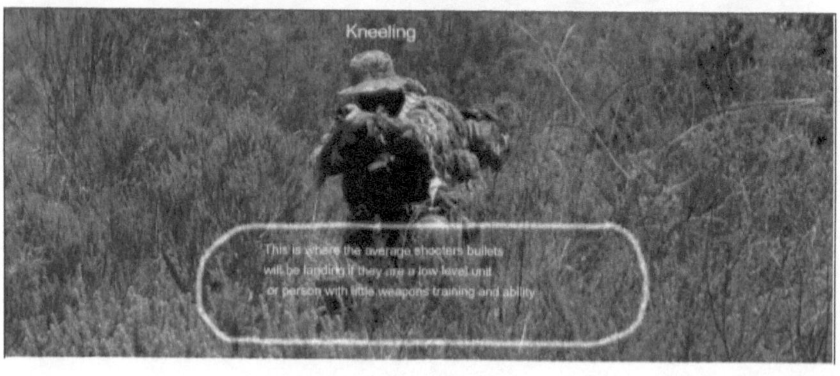
Kneeling
This is where the average shooters bullets
will be landing if they are a low level unit
or person with little weapons training and ability

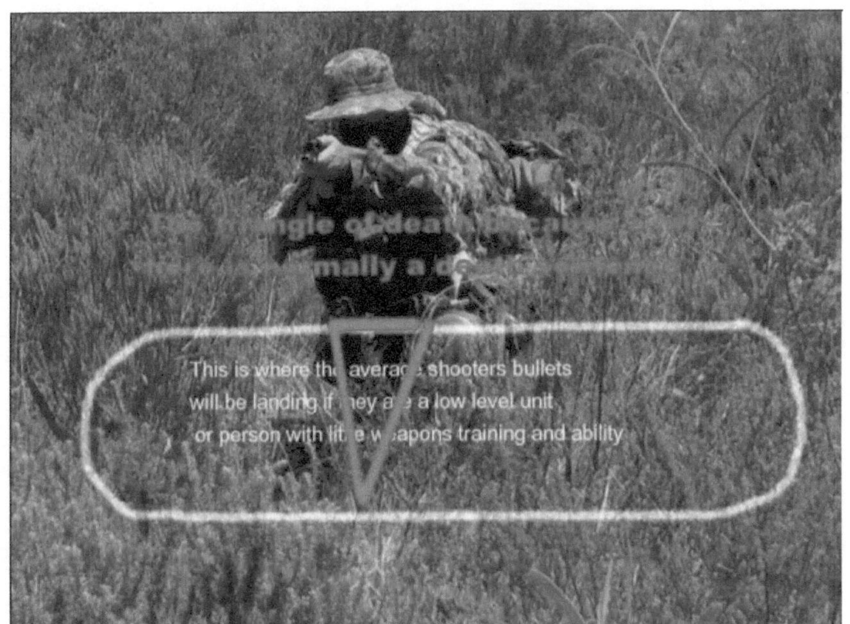
ngle of death
mally a d
This is where the average shooters bullets
will be landing if they are a low level unit
or person with little weapons training and ability

Key Aspects of Combat

The stress of combat

The stress created by a combat situation is the response that a combat situation elicits from you, and your ability to control or minimize the body's response will **determine your success or failure to an extent**. To an extent, because you can't stop a well-aimed bullet with just mindset – it involves a few factors and, at some point, your decision-making process will be overcome by the intensity (call it confusion or fog of war), what I mean is your ability to change mentally and physically to the dynamic situation of combat. If you allow fear to overpower you, then you could lose the confrontation due to its debilitating effects e.g., fear, anger, confusion, excitement or loss of focus are all part of the combat experience. Don't let these things control you, especially **fear** or **too much excitement** – stay focused on relaxation, breathe deep. This can and should be **trained consistently to a point where it is a reflex.**

The amount that the fear affects you is determined by the amount of training you have done and your experiences when training. This doesn't mean you won't have an adrenaline dump as fear and adrenaline are not necessarily associated. You can get the adrenaline dump from the thought of potential action or the thought of you dealing with pain or danger. Therefore, diminishing such thought patterns is a way to diminish the adrenaline effect.

Visualizing winning in your training sessions under **high pressure training** is how you condition your mind and body to relax when under stress. When training your body, the mental conditioning that you apply (mindset) in your mind as you are training is going to condition both your body to fight and your mind to win. This confidence that you build both mentally and physically translates into how you will fare and feel in a real-life situation to a degree because the adrenaline will affect you to some extent, which diminishes your ability some. Keep in mind a highly trained individual is less likely to be affected to the same extent by the negative effects of adrenaline (adrenal dump, auditory exclusion and fixation) than an untrained person.

Some aspects of your preparation for combat work both ways, such as *deep breathing* which allows you to relax. When your body is relaxed you can breathe normally and this allows your mind to work better and think better which allows you to win in a combat situation which will allow you to relax even more and therefore your breathing will be more relaxed, relaxing your body even more. This is what brings you into a combat master zone of relaxation and focus (joy/exhilaration). This is why a professional fighter that has had 30 or 40 professional fights seems so much more relaxed than a new fighter, it is the ingrained reflex and experience of combat which allows the mind to relax and the body follows.

But don't be fooled – a professional fighter can be overcome by being too old and slow to use the experience he has learned so don't get too carried away or phased by an older experienced fighter, you still need your speed and agility to be good at combat. Where a more experienced fighter can win in a situation is through superior mindset and timing, by timing I mean he can foresee and react quicker than you because of experience. Good timing comes with experience and an ability to read the enemy. This might be less relevant in a situation where skills are the overarching element for victory e.g., in the case of speed and accuracy with a pistol or rifle, the deciding factor will be dexterity with the firearm which doesn't take a lot of fitness or power or athletic ability.

Any person who takes winning in a combat situation seriously **goes through scenarios in their mind** as to what they will do in an event of something happening. This helps the mind to think strategically, gives your mind something to work with in a combat environment. It makes you more familiar with strategic planning, and practice makes perfect. Strategic planning is another skill that your mind can learn to do better and faster with experience, as your mind is able to come to a conclusion about the veracity of your actions in any specific option quicker.

Mental and **physical** conditioning prevents this negative physical reaction to events that precipitates from the mind, which in turn causes the adrenal dump which can be out of fear. This response is due to the stress of combat (danger and potential pain), and, to an extent, conditioning of the mind over years through negative aspects of combat and crime (threats) can cause excessive stress associated with violence. This can be overcome and is achieved through visualization exercises. This is also overcome by doing physical drills, continuous repetition of a movement while you apply the mindset and relaxation techniques that you were taught, to keep your *body relaxed* and your *mind focused.*

The mental and physical association is what can either debilitate you or make you a winner. It is not so easy to just tell a person how the mental aspects affects the physical but they have to apply these aspects to know and understand how they work, as well as apply them in combat. So, the closest thing to combat will be training, therefore it's up to the instructor to design course material and scenarios which bring the abilities out of the student.

One very debilitating aspect applied in some training courses is the stress test or stress inducer. If this is *done at the wrong time* during the training phase for the student's development then you will end up with a person that feels **stress just by the thought of a combat** scenario. This is clearly very bad for the student in real combat as it will diminish their ability to perform under combat conditions. The student needs to first be introduced to the concepts of dealing with combat stress then trained in these techniques then months later they can be stressed in a scenario. Doing this too early will just make the student too excited to perform optimally. If the person wants to perform in a very violent and dynamic situation they will need to be trained correctly when it comes to stress management.

Your **mind and body** are conditioned through the **gradual increase** in **stress stimuli**, such as a larger partner to train with, more *realistic scenarios, intensity* in training such as *increase in speed of the movement* (maybe to failure depending on context) and intensity of the physical exercise (more reps and/or weight) in a gradual and ever-increasing way, demanding more from your body and mind. **A gradual increase is the secret**; don't try to go too fast initially or you may injure yourself, or lose *technical proficiency (technique)* and therefore **lose power**, *accuracy* and *efficiency*.

Remember *efficiency* is of the utmost importance in a combat situation as this produces power and, in the context of rifle shooting, speed of movement and accuracy to engage multiple targets. The efficiency is produced by using your core muscles to move and aim your weapon as they are large powerful muscles, which can move and stop your upper body the fastest. This is your shooting platform and your legs are your mobility. So keep this in mind – the core muscles aim and the legs move you; your eyes are for aiming and target acquisition.

Efficiency is the minimum amount of effort and strain for the maximum amount of effect, this applied in all forms of combat – unarmed, blade, pistol and rifle.

The stress from physical exertion and muscle fatigue which leads to **tiredness** is another aspect that can overcome your ability to concentrate and focus on the task at hand, and this is where efficiency normally breaks down due to fatigue. This is another area that needs to be addressed to be effective in fighting. This is when your fitness lets you down and you can't cope with the intensity or do the movement correctly any more. **Good technique** will allow you to still strike fairly hard, and shoot accurately even when you are tired.

You will notice mixed martial arts (MMA)/boxing fighters get diminished when they get tired, and can't execute a proper technique any more. One way to shoot more accurately when tired is to breathe in your lower abdomen; this stops your upper body from moving, because when the chest heaves it disrupts your aim. So, breathing into the abdomen is best and needs to be trained to be useful in combat.

NB: Good technique is very important to functioning once you are out of energy and fighting for your life. This is why you should focus on your technique till it doesn't break down when under stress. You don't really have a choice either stay calm or die.

The Complete Warrior

What makes a complete warrior or a more prepared fighter? There are some factors:

Movement skills and specific skills

How fast you move, when you move and direction

such as lateral skills, specific weapon skills such as magazine changes stoppage drills etc

Included is physical attributes strength, speed, power, agility etc

Tactical skills

How you use cover, how and when you change

mags, mechanical scanning how you scan and stay aware of your surroundings, the intensity of engaging

targets and how you deal with it e.g fast and accurate fire while moving

Peripheral

equipment layout where you put handgun or balde with layout of magazines and quality:holster, weapon,

blade Configuration of webbing and weapons

which effects accessability and efficiency. Use of NV (night hunting), Thermal, monocular (recce)

Mental skills

mental aspects of awareness , mindset, attitude, relaxed focus, unwavering confidence, trained consistently

and ingrained till second nature, can you deal with pressure and lack of sleep, do you know how to be relaxed yet alert

Preparation and type of training

Team drills or single operator focus of the programme, street based reality training or fantasy based training

Culmination:Realistic speed of exercise and stress induced to simulate reality of combat

trained by experience

Always train with people that have real life experience, having boxing or MMA doesn't mean real life because there are rules in Boxing

People that fought in a war and or in the street are not always but mostly the best to learn from

General security considerations and societal indoctrinations

To have peace in your society you have to discern fact from fiction, and it's pure fiction to think that taking away a person's ability to defend themselves will in any way help the crime situation. You would have to be totally corrupt or stupid to think this, yet people have been indoctrinated to believing this (disarming civilians such as in UK) is going to somehow make criminals less likely to attack and use a weapon against you. Time has borne this out – there are more knife attacks and even weapon (handgun) assaults in UK than in any time in history, this is directly as a result of the supposed weapons free society; the same happened in Australia.

No matter what type of excuse you use, it just doesn't make logical sense to hand over the decision of whether you live or die to an already criminally minded (sometimes insane) person. The facts show us that it is literally the worst thing you can do, as you leave criminals with weapons, as happened in UK, Australia, Germany, France (terrorists killed unarmed French citizens and those citizens were totally defenseless and they were made so by their government) etc. In fact, in Spain, Britain, Australia and France they had ***terrorist attacks that could have been stopped by an armed citizen.*** I would have a look at the agenda behind it and look at ***the people*** (the nation) behind it and make a decision on your plan of action, you will be surprised it will always be the same nation.

Thousands of lives have been lost due to the negligence of governments by disarming their citizens. Thereby leaving their citizens ***totally vulnerable to murder, rape and attack*** of any type and any mischief, which a criminal wants to bring against the law-abiding citizen. That means ***the responsibility of the government to protect its citizens by ensuring that they have the necessary capability to defend*** *themselves* was <u>stolen</u> **from them in Germany, France, United Kingdom** and other European countries. This is a sign that your country is run by evil and not righteous men. Since these countries have applied this to their citizens their criminality overall has increased massively, but even if this were not the case it still doesn't give the government the right to disarm citizens.

Interesting historical fact: when the Romans said to the Germans give us your swords, the Germans said NO *we won't be your slaves*. You wonder what the agenda behind the story is? If you take into consideration that after the European countries were disarmed, a certain group (nation) of people started pushing for bringing in third world savages and terrorists from Muslim countries.

Aspects of mental ability for effective combat

1. **Mindset**: Calm, Focused, Aggressive, Adapting
2. **Mental tools**: OAP (Observe, anticipate and plan)
3. **Mental rehearsal techniques**

Mindset is your attitude towards the combat situation and the opponent, that in turn affects your physical performance, whether negative or positive. For example, it could or should be a cold calculated anger with a focused mind that is alert to the opponent's movements, actions and position. You could also call the mindset a **focused (focused mind) and relaxed aggression.** This is the opposite of a wild uncontrolled anger that can get you killed if you lose control over your facilities.

Watching the opponent, you fight accordingly, this means a focused attention on their movements. You will notice some fighters have an uncanny ability to evade strikes even at a world class level; this is a **focused attention** able to detect subtle movements with a **relaxed body** (relaxed body of the fighter). Your mind cannot be busy with *any other thoughts* other than the enemy and your reaction to counter or nullify what they do and strike without thought (needs to be ingrained to unconscious level). This is only possible if you are relaxed and focused and react subconsciously – this must not be thought out but rather an instant reaction in order for it to work properly.

For example, consider a street mugging (non-ambush scenario). To react properly to an attacker, you need to observe the attacker and not think "ok now I am going to do this or that" as that will open you up to surprise attacks. Instead, you either **attack first** or **wait with an intense and focused mind** but **relaxed body. Let your body move without**

the conscious thought process – this will make you incredibly fast and unpredictable. This is only possible if you have done **thousands of repetitions** of the **proper** techniques beforehand, such as a reverse punch or in boxing what might be called a right cross. The same applies to shooting situations where the focus on the attackers and subconscious shooting techniques apply.

The repetition and confidence come from being able to do a technique against an opponent that is ready, and then it's easy against an enemy that is not ready for such a technique. If you decide to attack before he moves then it should be done with a relentless forward aggression, if in a situation where the only way out is to fight and winning is the only option.

Having explained how to observe the attacker, in a combat situation, I would suggest attack is the best way to conclude a combat situation, don't wait for him to attack you. If he is a good defensive fighter, you might run in to a strike or blade or a bullet – judge for yourself at the time when to get into action. *There are no rules in combat* so you can do whatever you feel needs to be done to conclude the situation. There is no such thing as a dirty fighting technique – only effective and ineffective techniques.

The mindset of a well-practiced warrior is to <u>**not**</u> think too much of specific techniques but to **allow the mind to instinctively come to the correct conclusion** of what should be done to win in a combat situation. This is understood as '**no mind**' in Japanese fighting teaching, but I would think that it is not a matter of having 'no thought process' but more to have **no specific technique in mind** – to react with what instinctively comes to mind. The more you train the correct technique and tactics the better your instinctive reaction will be. **The more you train** and the **better your quality of training** the **better will be your decision-making process.**

No system that teaches a particular technique for such and such an attack and a different technique for another attack, is going to be effective. By this I mean when you have 100 different attack angles and a 100 different defense options in some systems, your mind will be unable to search through all these – instead you need a simple solution for most attacks. Your mind might not be able to access the specific technique you were taught in class if there is a plethora of options, so **keep it simple**.

To put this in perspective, it will look like this: if an assailant wants to stab you, punch him in the face with correct technique and you have a great chance of winning; if he has a grenade, punch him in the face; if he has a pistol, punch him in the face after redirecting the barrel, and so on. Simple and proven effective this is direct and easy to learn. I have used it so many times I have lost count. It works and there are no doubts if you know how to punch you can be 90% effective. You can't be 100% sure because you never know who you are fighting such as a maybe a boxer who can take a punch.

Combat is too flexible (varied) for that type of rigid mindset. You must have done thousands of repetitions of movement, drawing of your weapon, striking and manipulation. I find it much more useful to teach an understanding of combat and then do simple techniques that can be applied in multiple scenarios. For example, do thousands of repetitions of techniques known to actually work in realistic combat scenarios, then teach the mindset of being calm but aggressive.

You should be moving in a dynamic way that is smooth and balanced, with no specific thoughts, thereby allowing your mind to reach an instinctive reaction (conclusion) to an attack. Your primary goal is to switch off the control of the attacker's body, which is via his brain. This is better done with superior accuracy with reasonable speed and intensity.

This is not always possible as you sometimes barely have time to ID (identify) the attacker, you will be presenting a weapon and shooting in maybe 1.5-2 sec (highly trained shooters can draw and shoot in under a 1 sec, but the shock factor can sometimes mitigate this). That means you are grateful to get center mass shots on target as time will sometimes only allow for this, and some of the time you will be grateful to even get a hit on target at all, if the attack is totally unexpected. This is because your brain is first trying to identify whether it's a problem or not and then it's trying to identify the attacker. These factors make it difficult to act immediately and this causes a delay in reaction by you to the attack. This is one of the reasons attacks are so successful as the attackers have such an advantage over anyone untrained and unsuspecting.

Righteous thought patterns promote survival

Understanding why you fight or defend your family and friends is very important in righteous action. This is because any hesitation can get you killed and *seconds count* so *determine this beforehand.*

If you are wondering about whether you should be carrying a blade/or the modern day equivalent the pistol then go read Luke Chapter 22 verse 36 in the Christian Bible. One of the reasons or a contributing factor is the inculcated mindset of having no weapon is somehow beneficial to survival; this has been introduced by the communists in the school system and universities. This is a contributing factor but not the only reason we have such a massive crime rate in South Africa, the mindset indoctrinated and inculcated by the universities and learning institutions backed and sponsored by people and organization with a lack of respect of GOD, and our GOD given right to self-defense. This brings about the misunderstanding that if you are not armed then criminals will be nice to you. This is **fantasy of the highest order**, because you are more likely to lose your life if you have no way of defending yourself. This is happening so many times all around where these people are working on making people really dumb to reality. Thousands of people die in these countries because their governments are taken over by shadow groups behind the scenes.

Basically, the criminals can't believe what a fool you are to be unarmed, it's so much easier for them to steal from an unarmed citizen that an armed citizen. Think about it – if you were a criminal, **would you want to attack an armed person** or an unarmed one?

The South African government seems to be more occupied with the law-abiding citizen as it has not occurred to them that it is the criminals that are involved with crime. It's what is called "when your gardener becomes your president", a distinctly African problem.

It's a difficult one to work out especially for the head of the police; he thinks having law abiding citizens unarmed might help? And of course, the police don't mind arming the criminals or gangs, basically the criminals are an extension of the government (as our governing party was once listed as a terrorist organization).

To **not** be a target in combat/SHTF type scenario, you need at least 3 of the following (if you have all 6 of these points trained in or part of your character then you are a hard target):

1. A weapon, not obvious or openly as this can attract trained or desperate individuals
2. Training, in intensity, speed and accuracy under duress
3. Correct mindset
4. Awareness
5. Decisive, aggressive and rapid reactions
6. Assess your environment and your performance and at a later date correct any shortcomings.

The psychology of winning and science of victory

Correct training principles bring about a positive mindset by experience and conditioning of the mind and body as a unit. This is through experience of techniques working in training and therefore the winning mindset is reinforced. Furthermore, using your techniques in varied situations further reinforces this correct mindset. This is due to the decision-making process that you need to work through when you are presented with multiple options to choose from and can make good decisions leading to a reasonable outcome.

The techniques need to be **trained to instinct** (repetition of the correct technique). *Techniques that are understood and can be applied without conscious thought*, and are applicable to real life situations, will be useful for self-protection, taking into consideration how people attack, in particular the intensity and forward momentum of the attack. As well as understanding how people react when being shot. It's not always as you think it might be as some people barely show a response at all and some drop like a stone. It's got to do with shot placement and the psychology of the individual that dictates how they react to the impact.

To **train something to an instinctive level**, it is recommended you do at least **4000 repetitions** to be able to apply a specific technique in a real situation. Keep in mind, also ingrain the mindset that goes with combat. The number of repetitions to acquire high levels of skill is only a generalization – it could be far less for a person with natural inclination for martial prowess, but on average it's going to take a lot of repetition. I have seen where some people take a year to reach a fairly high standard and then can go on to train themselves and they get really good with the foundational understanding inculcated of what constitutes a good tactic technique and procedure to prevail in combat.

Mindset and how the brain affects your actions

The mind can either assist or detract from your ability to function in a fight. That is why we focus a lot on the mental attitude of the student and constantly reinforce the "mindset" attitude.

A misunderstood concept is that you have muscle memory; this is incorrect because your muscle cannot remember, but what does happen is the information stored in the cerebellum (repetition allows neural pathways to be ingrained) is more easily accessible to you in a fight if you have done enough repetitions for this information to become more of a subconscious function than a thought-out action. So, a more appropriate term for this function is to say how to develop subconscious memory function or stress memory function and this is found in the cerebral cortex which is closer to the nerves of the body than the actual brain.

This area is closest to your spinal column which allows your body to access the information quicker than an untrained person. It will also have something to do with the brain's understanding of the movements of an attacker, how it looks (how the brain interprets the movement) for a person to attack and the *subtle signs* a person's body will give off before an attack, these will also speed up your reaction to an attack.

This is because you are reacting to subtle signs that another person might not pick up, this is the same for sparring with a person that has very little training and you might be a 'black belt' that allows you to see what others can't see. An experienced fighter knows a lot about the subject of combat and can see the subtle signs. For example, in a "street" situation, this might be as subtle as picking up an opponent's front foot moving first, because you can see their whole body, due to relaxation and a 'soft' (wide view) visual focus technique. This small and subtle sign helps you to move first or simultaneously. If too much tension is present, your pupil will constrict and the field of view will change and narrow everything down, hurting your chances.

The reality of how your mind reacts to stress is dictated by the **amount** of training, time period of training, intensity of training and the *quality* and number of repetitions you have done during training. The quality of your training will lead to fast accuracy and this is what brings about the confidence.

Quality also refers to the training received with regards to **reality-based tactics, techniques and procedures** as opposed to training based on a figment of someone's imagination. Never underestimate the importance of the flexible mindset training. You will also realize as you gain experience with teaching is that *good technique* seems to stay with the student and there is *little loss in accuracy* even *after a long time of abstinence* from training.

This is only applicable if you have adequate training to override all other natural responses that might have been in your subconscious. Bad or inadequate technique tends to leave you with bad accuracy after a hiatus in your training such as a year or 2 of abstinence. It does take time to develop these skills to the level where they are subconscious but once you reach this level then you will more likely hold onto them for a long time. What will happen though is you will lose speed and accuracy as these tend to degrade with time if you don't practice them consistently.

Has the instructor taken into consideration the time-distance relationship e.g., can the technique you are doing have the ability to fit into the time it takes for the attacker to attack you? An illustration of this would be making 2 or 3 moves in the time the attacker does one downward strike with a blade. **Logic** says this would be impractical (even impossible) in real life fighting situations, this is because there is a maximum speed with which you can move your limbs. This means if he is moving at maximum speed and you are moving at maximum speed, this is within reason a boundary for speed and can only overcome with extensive training for speed and superior mindset. This will even have its limits due to the reduced ability that is induced by adrenaline (tension/fear).

Does it fit into *full speed training* and can the technique still be applied? That's why what is done in combat varies to what is taught in the classroom or training range. The further away from real war the military of a country is, the more fanciful the training becomes due to human nature, and the danger and nature of real combat training are lost in time. It could also be due to influx of persons involved with the training that do not have the necessary combat experience, which leads to fanciful training strategies.

Highly trained warriors do not experience the fight or flight symptoms **to the same extent** as an untrained person would. It might be that some of the symptoms will affect the trained warrior but **not to the same extent** and sometimes very little if at all depending on the extent of the confrontation and the training that was done by the defender (operator). This can also be affected by the length of time since training seriously for combat, if it's still fresh in your mind and your body is in good condition then you should deal well with an attack with greater ease than if you were unfit.

If you don't have time to think about an attack and it happens out of the blue, then you tend to react well if your training for combat is comprehensive and intense enough that your mind works in the attack level of intensity. This is probably because the mind and body function subconsciously to come to a defense strategy and there is no time to clutter the mind with irrelevant thoughts.

The instructor should at certain intervals, reinforce mindset and incorporate exercises to make the student more aware of their mindset and help to reinforce the process of consciously relaxing, breathing deeply, staying confident, thinking of what they must do and **not the attacker can do to harm them.** It will behoove (appropriate) you to have this mindset and to do the same on your course during training, or even when you train on your own reinforcing and using your mindset with tactics or procedures that will help you in a fight. This doesn't mean you don't watch the enemy with focus and relaxed attention, as what they do will determine your reaction to an extent. It's just that your mind cannot be focused on unnecessary thoughts if you want to survive a contact.

Situational Awareness

Awareness is the ability to observe the environment around you and calculate or determine to an extent what is going on and how it will affect you as an individual or a team, and then act on that information correctly to overcome the problem that presents itself. In self-defense, this could be seeing a group of possible attackers then making a plan and acting on it. In a military context it could be noticing an ambush or indications of an ambush such as enemy equipment (footprints, camp fire smell), and then taking the appropriate action to nullify the ambush or break through it and so on.

1. This is the very beginning of any type of self-defense or military function where you work in a small or large team. This is because understanding the position of where the enemy is compared to your position is very important to succeeding in combat. This and understanding the enemy's disposition with regards to weapons and equipment etc.

2. You can have all the training in the world but that cannot help you if you are not aware of your surroundings. "In the street" it's mostly about the criminal element. In a military situation it's about a lot more than just the enemy, it's about terrain, your enemy's capability, your personal situation (readiness), friendlies and enemy assets etc.

3. Area awareness
    a. Immediate area awareness is essential to combat survival, personal survival (self-defense) and other areas such as escape and evasion. This is so that you know which direction your enemy is, and how close they are will dictate how and what you use to defend yourself with.
    b. Extended area awareness is essential for planning

immediate actions and preparation, you need extended awareness for temporary bases, hold up points and so on, this is normal done with OP/LP (listening post or observation post) but can also be done with binocular (terrain allowing)/ monocular /spotting scope. Another way of achieving wider areas awareness is the drone, which can do a 360 degree around your LP/OP or temporary base.

4. Long term awareness of potential scenarios with regards to the enemy disposition and intentions will also play a major role, but we are mainly concerned with situational awareness here as to your combat environment. This being the immediate danger to you and therefore the situation as it unfolds around you at the point in time.

5. Every person in your team, that means <u>every single person,</u> is an intelligence gatherer and creates your situational awareness. This is done by constantly feeding information to each other as you move through the terrain.

6. Increasing situational awareness **using technology**, this could be

   a. Small drone
   b. Night Vision (NV) technology (scope or monocular)
   c. Thermal scope or monocular
   d. Possibly a range finder to estimate or know fairly accurately how far the enemy is with regards to your position.
   e. More crudely you could use nylon tied as 'trip wire' to a soda can with pebbles in that shake as a person disturbs the can if they walk into the nylon. The nylon could run through/ around your area and the can be inside your hide so as to only alert you.

*A*wareness is only **valuable if** it is **coupled with calculation** (planning) and the correct actions, such as a correct attack, aggressive counter ambush (attacking an ambush), or tactical withdrawal (moving away with covering fire), or attack and withdrawal. It could also mean just staying still to allow the enemy to pass, especially in a 'reconnaissance' purpose or objective in the context of a listening post in a war (non-permissive environment) or in the context of "the street" negating a possible mugging, by taking another route to bypass a possible criminal party. So awareness is essential in a combat environment including self-defense in the street.

There are **<u>no varying levels or degrees of awareness</u>** – you are either *aware or not*. Once you are aware, this then leads to observing the attacker and deciding what you will do (this is the planning phase of OAP), this then changes to a combat mindset, which is a cold aggression. To say there are levels of awareness means you know when trouble is about to strike, and also that there are times when you don't have to be fully aware. Common sense tells you that awareness is a mindset that should always be present while you are awake and that you only relax when you are asleep. Think of it as a sense of awareness, yet with a relaxed disposition (character) of the body, and this will become second nature to you.

It is not a tense and furtive disposition but a relaxed and calm awareness (cognizance); you take in the environmental stimulus and calculate the possibilities of how the world might change around you. A relaxed disposition and demeanour allow the mind to flirt over the myriad of possibilities, this might even be subconscious in some aspects and this is called your sixth sense, which is made keener through experience.

OAP = awareness (i.e., consider "observe anticipate plan" as being an acronym for "awareness"). This gives you a way of dealing with your environment:

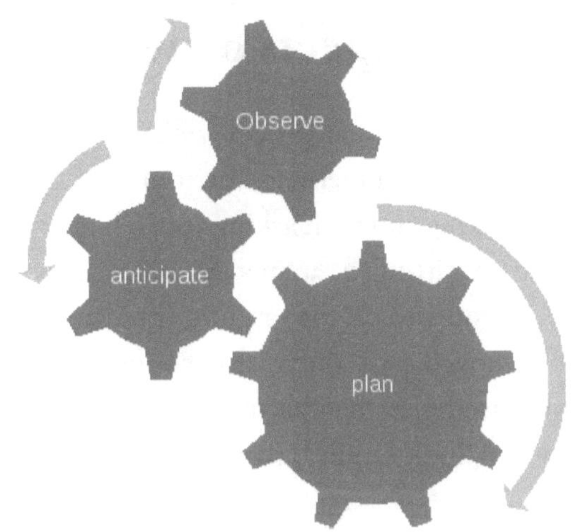

Observe
anticipate
plan

Aspects of awareness

Awareness is a continual process of looking and calculating what is happening in your immediate environment. Awareness is the mental process of looking and then asking yourself questions e.g., why a person is standing or sitting in a specific place. Do they pay unnecessary attention to you and do they mimic your movements? Did they move off as you moved past them, this could be coincidence or planned. Once your awareness has become second nature and you don't have to consciously look around, then it has become part of your everyday functions.

Awareness starts a decision-making process. Self-defense will most likely apply to areas that are built up such as towns because they are where you will most likely find various criminal elements, this will be due to abundance of targets for such criminals.

A questioning mindset is a calculating mind, calculating leads to assessment and this leads to planning and the quality of plan will be dictated by your experience and quality of your training. ***The following example questions to ask yourself when observing your environment apply more to a self-defense/combat situation:***

- Is it normal for a person to stand in a particular location where you've observed someone?
- Why are those 3 people looking around nervously, possibly communicating with each other?
- Why are those guys communicating surreptitiously over the road to each other by looking around and then at each other?
- Should that person be dressed so warmly in such a hot climate?
- Did they follow me as I passed by and then turn when I turned?
- Why are those individuals just standing around, with no

obvious purpose?

Questions concerning awareness for SHTF conflict will be slightly different; here it could be in the countryside or towns

- Depending on the terrain your questions might address 'sign' left by people moving through your area of operations such as spoor (footprints). Here you would want to know how many people there were, their direction of travel, signs of weapons (equipment left behind or imprint of stock where person leant weapon against a tree), fires, broken branches from moving through, grass trampled down etc.
- Open terrain, such as we would find in farm land or bushveld, would mean looking for observation points people might take for OP/LP, farm houses, any man-made structure, camp sites (in SHTF they might be a danger but in normal situation they won't). It will be similar to your military operations because of the terrain, the difference is in a civil unrest situation (SHTF) even civilians might be potential enemies.
- Because of the lack of crowds, it would be much more obvious if there were people in the area and they would stand out and anybody in the area would attract your attention and you would ask yourself what their purpose was and a period of approximately 1 hour will give you some indication of what they are doing in the area. That is if you have time to observe them, as your object might be purely a distraction which means it would be irrelevant, unless you are looking for some equipment that they might have or food or water.
- Another aspect of traveling in open (rural) environments would be looking for shelter/cover when you need to stop and rest. Depending on the type of situation security considerations will be relevant especially in a SHTF type

scenario. The shelter would preferably be close to water and have a high point to look over the land from as well as avenues of escape.

- Questions that might come to mind in a combat environment when occupying your shelter and when observing the movement of potential combatants will be if they are tracking you or just happen to be in the area. Either way your pack should be packed or ready to go, so don't unpack until you are sure you are in a fairly safe area. Only take out what you need at that time e.g., food and water.
- Open terrain has more potential for an all-out attack by a party as in an urban environment where they have to potentially contend with the police or other bystanders. This will be negated by the fact that you will most probably be moving with a long gun in semi auto.

Key points in awareness

1. *Question how people are acting in relation to their environment and to you.* Normally potentially hostile individuals would be moving quickly (or quicker than the rest of the public) if in a following (tracking) context and they would be looking around for witnesses, possibly reaching for something in their pockets (this can also be checking to reassure themselves e.g., that their knife/gun is still there), looking at someone to communicate. Such signs could be the precursor to an attack or a possible intention to attack, whether it is carried through or not.

2. *Study the body language of people.* This might differ slightly for different cultures but the base stuff still stays the same. Some cultures are more excitable and use their hands more, for example the Italians are more volatile and expressive. Arabic culture is also more excitable than western cultures as is Israeli which is the cousin of the Arab, you could quiet easily think there was a major argument going on in a street in Jerusalem, this might be a minor disagreement. Keep this in mind. The Germans are more subdued and calmer, if you saw Germans acting like Italians then you would be alarmed. General body language signs of tension examples are: are their **shoulders hunched or fist clenched** or are their **hands holding something which could be a weapon** and generally being furtive (eyes moving faster than normal) with **eyes move side to side (this might not be obvious but observable)?** These signs could be the precursor to an attack. You will have to be close to see many additional signs e.g., pupil dilatation in the eyes could be from adrenaline or drugs – either way that could mean danger to you. Keep in mind people who are up to something no good will have a certain

tension about them that is visible if you know what to look for.

3. **Use your *peripheral vision*** at all times, especially while walking or moving through buildings and doors. This helps to pick up a person approaching from the side, especially quick movement should be quite apparent to your peripheral vision. Looking backwards and using your peripheral vision you can detect quick movement. This is a very valuable tool for scanning 360 degrees around you and should become part of your everyday habits.

4. When walking, turning your head and using your peripheral vision allows you to see behind you if someone is following or moving in quickly to close the gap between you and them. They will be more visible to you because they are moving faster than the surrounding foot traffic. **See diagram below** for the "360-degree scan" technique.

5. Looking ***close*** and ***far*** helps to control an area more effectively with visual observation. Close can be doorways and such, and far can be vehicles in the distance, bushes, trees, parks (places where criminals can hang out without being disturbed). Be especially aware when leaving your vehicle/home arriving back at your vehicle/home, and going in/out of a shop/restaurant/similar.

6. Looking ***slightly down*** when surrounded gives you a better view of who is around you and where they are placed (this is if they are standing fairly close to you 1-5 meters). You would not be standing around if they were armed with weapons such as handguns and rifles as this would be a death sentence, you need to shoot and or move fast while shooting or just moving fast, shooting and moving is far superior because of the shock factor that causes the enemy to miss and run.

7. Remember, **do not ignore that feeling you get about a**

situation (**sixth sense**), but can't explain what it is, a feeling that the situation 'is not right'. Don't ignore it because this is a capability God gave you to asses a situation *subconsciously* to protect you from danger. Don't listen to nonsense about how such techniques evolved over trillions of years – leave fantasy for children's books. It's part of your programming by the Master builder and programmer, Himself.

Exercise to train awareness

- This should be done at a low intensity to avoid injury
- It is a **mental exercise** and not an intensity exercise
- This will increase your decision-making process and tactics
- It will allow you to use your peripheral vision more efficiently

Stand with 3 or 4 people (potential assailants) around the student and each such person can have a different type of training weapon (e.g., plastic knife or handgun). Such weapons could include a handgun, knife, or baton/impact weapon; and something non-lethal such as a cell phone. The idea is to force you to make quick decisions as to which person to engage. This is a mental process so you can even use your fingers to point at the person who you think is the most dangerous to you and which one you would engage in order of importance as to which attacker poses the greatest threat. It is also an awareness process so watching as many of the individuals as possible is part of the exercise and this should help with awareness in general.

1. ***This is more important than you think so don't ignore this exercise.***
2. Attackers can initially only present their weapons and the student must decide which person he/she would neutralize first. They could even use a finger just to point at the opponent, because it's a mental exercise not a shooting one.
3. Then extend the drill by allowing the surrounding people to move towards the student slowly, as this will also force the student to decide which the priority person to stop first is and which weapon is more dangerous at which range.

The "360° scan" technique

The following diagram illustrates what is meant earlier above about using your peripheral vision. Here NV stand for normal vision and PV stands for peripheral vision. In the diagram below we have a view from the top of how you turn your head and use your peripheral vision to scan the area behind you, to front and sides.

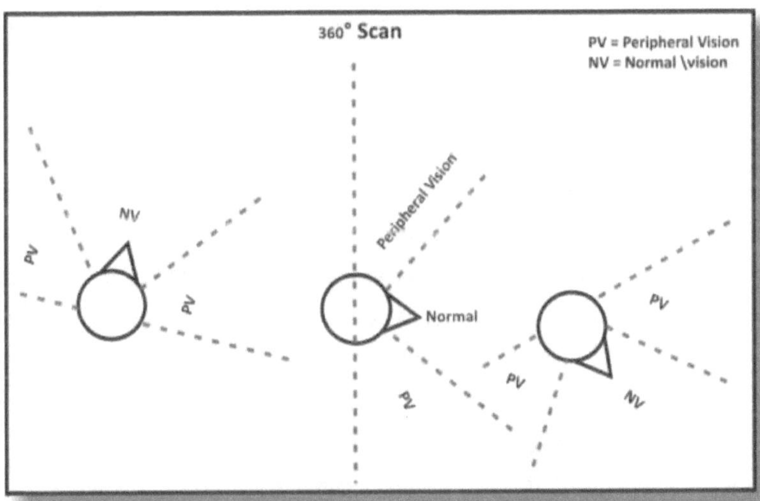

An example of awareness in action

Imagine you are a woman and looking around in an urban setting and notice a guy standing doing nothing, just watching everybody (trying to act casual), with his shoulders hunched and he's looking slightly tense. This scenario could happen many times as you are walking around during the day or night. Your observation becomes a casual way of assessing your environment.

You decide to access your blade *covertly* as you walk past or up an alley. You realize the person followed you, so you turn keeping the blade away from the attacker so they can't see it or grab your arm to try to disarm you or stop you using your hand with the blade in it.

The attacker lunges for your necklace and you deflect the attack and proceed to *incapacitate* the attacker with your weapon. Keep in mind this could mean going from fist to blade and then to pistol. Depending on what you instinctively feel is appropriate for the context, this will always be your choice and should be encouraged by the instructor to give you the confidence and ability to deal with a combat situation.

You assess the situation once you have incapacitated your attacker and observe your surroundings to see if there are any more attackers and if there is a way to escape for you. **You then leave the area to a safer environment.**

Motivation to defend yourself must be **settled before the combat starts,** don't go into a fight half-heartedly, **as this will get you killed.** If you decide to fight do so with **total commitment and ferocity. This might seem like a minor matter** but it's actually imperative because *any hesitation* in the street could get you killed, so deciding beforehand whether you have the skill and commitment to deal with a life and death encounter is very important. Combining this with a righteous mindset and motivation is very important.

Training Principles For Teaching Combat

Keep in mind when reading this manual that for the sake of brevity we cannot cover all areas or aspects of weapon use and every type and technique with regards to weapon retention or disarming, as the manual would just be too long. I have tried to keep it simple and with only the essentials for combat and survival in single operator situations. If you have very little time available to train then ***train the basics*** as these will keep you alive in most situations. You really only need to be fast and accurate and this will stand you in good stead for most combat situations. I have specified the basics for good combat ability below, as they are the most critical for combat efficiency.

The principles of effective training

Knowing and understanding the ***basics of the specific discipline*** you want to learn is what makes you good at that discipline.

It is said that **to be a master** in a specific discipline you need to do at least **10 000 hours** of training, but this is not as simple in self-defense because the person will have to spend 10 000 hours **of the correct techniques, tactics** and **mindset** to be a master at combat, as these are essential to success. Personally, I think that it is a bit of an exaggeration as I have seen people get very proficient in pistol and rifle with 3-4 hours training on weekends over a period of about 1-2 years. It also won't help you to have 10 000 hours of kung-Fu, because we have seen supposed masters getting beaten by an MMA fighter with much less hours of training than the master. There is a reason for this and it is that some systems are not geared for combat. A more accurate amount of time to become proficient with a weapon for self-defense is probably closer to 300-600 hours of training and 3-6 years. What can speed up the process is correct and realistic training techniques that actually work with a good understanding being imparted to the student.

As with all things in life the number of hours the person will have to practice will depend largely on the person who's being taught, it could be a lot less than 10 000 hours, it might be as low as ***500 hours*** for some. Note that you might not be a master of combat but you can have ***excellent skills***. From my experience, a person can have exceptional expertise and skill with 4-8 hors training a week over a period of 3-6 years depending on the person's age, athleticism, time available to train, motivation, focus and intelligence.

Realize that a person can have useful wisdom, and yet lack technical proficiency and understanding of certain aspects of mechanically operated devices. We can think of such people as having positive "street smarts" but perhaps lacking certain academic skills.

Do not allow **negative thoughts** to dominate your thinking, as *they will affect your performance* negatively through subtle tension building up in your body. Instead, focus on strategy and moving to your advantage. Even better than thinking of strategy is to have a predetermined combat strategy that is simple and effective. Negative thoughts are usually as a result of previous experience (bad situations) and lack of preparation. Negative thoughts will tense you up and cause you to slow down; this can be debilitating and should be avoided at all costs.

Expect to win and use positive reinforcement continually. This is done until it becomes second nature. Do this in training so that you more than likely do it in a real-life situation.

Stay mentally focused but **physically relaxed**. This means the mind is focused and adapting to what the enemy is doing and the body is relaxed to move fast and think better. Watch people and the situation around you carefully, using the acronym OAP (as explained earlier). Awareness gives you a few seconds longer to react if you notice any attackers and allows you to mentally prepare or brace even if it's only a second or two.

Remember **every** (**not some**) **opponent has a weakness** and is to some degree apprehensive of you whether they show it or not. It's the person that ignores and overrides these feelings and replaces them with either excitement or positive thoughts that stands the most chance of winning. Laughing is a good way to relax and fight better, try it next time and you will be amazed. The attacker might think you are insane and become unsettled; it's unnerving to see someone that could die any second smiling or laughing at this point in time, think carefully about that. Any time an attacker is scared gives you the advantage, let that sink in ☺ .

Perhaps use a key word or a phrase to get your mind into a focused mode e.g., if you're facing muggers or any enemy think something like "breathe deep" or whatever your "go to" word is, you might even exclaim it outwardly. This is not essential because you can just breathe deeply and consciously relax your body to get focused. Focus is a state of being **physically relaxed** and mentally **aware of your surroundings (environment) and attacker.**

Reduce the stress you experience by applying visualization exercises during your training i.e., before any combat situation arises. This is because in your visualization you will overcome and win and this will set you up with a better mindset. Correctly applied visualization will have a lot of detail in it to bring about the desired result. It should be done daily for a couple of months to prepare your mind for combat. Training with a combat mindset with the correct focus on physical and mental aspects prepares you for combat.

Use fewer techniques and *become proficient in these techniques* to bring your reaction time down. The reason your reaction time will be faster is because your mind will have a basic response to most attacks and this will help you be less confused as to a plan of action. Confusion is your enemy, so *simplicity of tactic and technique* is therefore your friend, as is instant reaction to an attack. To win with your firearm, you need a good "center mass" hit that causes incapacitation quickly which is not the same for every person except in cases where a brain stem shot is executed. A quick and accurate draw or presentation of the rifle with a well-placed incapacitating shot is what it takes.

For example: awareness means you can ID the attacker (that's the OAP = observe anticipate plan, which is a mental tool), you then move laterally, draw your firearm simultaneously, ID the target as the person might either not be an attacker or even an innocent (or who may not be the attacker you saw earlier in a prolonged situation), engage if the person turns out to be the enemy, then check your environment. This will increase your confidence when you are able to quickly and efficiently do target identification.

Here is another example of what I mean in a context of a street fight, of course it takes a good bit of time to perfect your striking technique, but once you have it you will and can keep it for life, your defense strategy looks like this: strike to the ***groin, knee to the head***, then finish with a more deadly (incapacitating) strike such as a throat strike or eye jab or rear of the ***neck strike***. The neck, especially the rear of the neck, is filled with nerves and the spine with smaller and more delicate bones than the rest of the spine and is very vulnerable to a strike with the ulna bone of the forearm which is a fairly strong bone and is capable of causing pain and incapacitating a person.

This is especially important when faced with a close opponent where you can't draw your pistol immediately as this might allow the attacker to grab your weapon. I remember a particularly successful strike to the back of the neck when grabbed by someone in an alley when 5 men failed in their attempt to mug me. That one strike gave me the ascendancy, instantly incapacitating my nearest attacker, and they quickly realized it was futile to continue their attack once I could draw my knife to counter their knives.

Keeping your techniques to a minimum also allows you to train those aspects of your combat strategy more than if you try to learn 50 ways to disarm a blade or gun. This doesn't mean just one technique but more an understanding of ***how and why a technique works*** and then allowing a certain amount of flexibility as each person is different and getting them to adapt is of great importance. Anecdotal evidence is the fact that in the 70 street situations 60-70 % of the time a simple fast and accurate punch can finish the fight, keep in mind they were not raving lunatics high on some drug.

Keeping the number of techniques to a minimum

1. This will give you more time for the ***basics.***
2. You can do more repetitions of those techniques you know work.
3. Less fatigue due to hours needed to get good at basic technique.

4. Less chance of injury as its easier to learn and apply one basic technique, the more you do the technique the better.
5. You will have a more in-depth understanding of the techniques you know with more intimacy. This will lead to more accuracy over the long run, don't change your technique every few months as you set yourself back more than you realize.
6. Doing the **basics perfectly** is what makes you good which leads to mastery and deadly accuracy.
7. More time for those essential techniques that are proven to be effective, the secret is getting training from someone who knows the difference between techniques that work and these that don't.

Attitudes and expectations can play a role in your performance so a positive attitude will mostly bring about a positive outcome as far as this is humanly possible and your training has allowed for the performance that will be needed. Performance is dictated by speed, agility, accuracy, mobility combined with strategy and mindset.

Objective of training principles for combat rifle

This is to prepare the student for physical confrontation in the street/war zone, in a survival situation or in an attack in any theatre of operations. The techniques and tactics are not all expedient for teams but in some cases can be used for team members; if all the members of the team train together and ***understand the dynamic nature of the techniques then it is possible to use them for combat teams.***

Is it better to know yourself or to know your enemy, which is more important?

Both are equally important: know yourself, weaknesses and strong points, change habits that are bad for your combat ability. And know your enemy's weak points and tactics and techniques, as in this way you can plan how to defeat them before you even make contact.

General overview of training principles

Fallacies about combat training

Here is a list of common fallacies regarding training:

1. **You can do a 3-day weapons course and you will be effective.** In **reality,** it takes **years** to get really good and there is **no shortcut to excellence.**

   a. To get a reasonable understanding of **unarmed combat, blade, pistol** or **rifle** should take the average student about 2 to 4 hours per week per subject for 3 years. So, if each subject is given 4 hours per week and there are 4 subjects then you could say it will take at least 2 hrs. x 52 weeks x 3 years x 4 subjects = 1248 hours of training to be good at all the 4 major subjects for self-defense. These are guidelines as different people learn at different rates and they have different background knowledge and physical capabilities, which either assists or detracts from the speed of learning. It is easier to learn pistol and rifle than it is to learn unarmed combat because of the fitness, speed, power, flexibility and strength required in unarmed combat.

   b. What really helps to speed up the process is to have a good understanding of what makes a person accurate (grip, stance, weapon presentation), mobile and dynamic and with correct mindset. The key is *concentrating on the basics* and drilling them to instinct and then only developing the more complex or advanced aspects when the person has the basics mastered.

   c. *A master is the person who has mastered the basics.*

2. **You can use any shooting stance and grip, with any arm position and they will all work equally well in combat.** Having said that the combat stance with one foot forward and the one foot backwards will be a little more stable and will allow more control for recoil. Even though some stances will work to an extent, you should find the technique which allows you to use the least energy (most efficient), cause the least fatigue and allow you to point with the rifle instinctively, finding your sights quickly for close and long ranges. *Any technique that causes stress or tension is probably wrong and will fatigue you out in the long run and is bad for real combat, as you should have as little tension induced by your technique as possible.* Here are realistic issues regarding stance and grip:

   a. We know from real life that a stance where the rifle stock is in the position of pressing on the shoulder does not perform as well positioning the stock on the pectoral muscles close to the sternum (center bone of chest) for 'instinctive' shooting. The latter allows better recoil management. This is due to the amount of weight behind the stock to control recoil – if someone pushes on your shoulder it's easier to move it off line, but if the person pushes on your center of mass then it is more difficult for them to destabilize you. It's a basic fact of physics that any force applied to the center of mass (center of gravity) does not alter the attitude (angle, position) of the object, it might merely move the object along the line of force. Whereas forces applied off-center do change the attitude, and in fact the further the force is away from the center, the more easily the object can be repositioned. In this case, the rifle recoil is the force, and shouldering the rifle too far from your center makes your fire very much less accurate, especially when using rapid shot sequences.

b. The centerline stock position increases your chances of survival because it has less to go wrong.

c. It's even better if your stock is **short enough** so you can put the stock in the middle of the pectoral muscles, as this then puts the rifle sight in line with your aiming eye and allows a more natural sight alignment with less stress on the neck muscles. This will allow you to go for a longer period without fatigue. This is another reason that "bull pup" style rifles are easier to manipulate than an assault rifle of standard design.

d. The rifle can also be brought higher so the stock is fairly high on the pectoral muscles, which means you don't have to lower your head too much and put stress on the neck muscles. Staining too much will cause tension and the tension will cause fatigue.

3. **If you train hard enough you can fight effectively against a person with a gun or blade while you are unarmed.** While this is possible, your chances of survival are minimal. Avoid unarmed combat because the percentage chances of success are 10-20% or less depending on your skill level (strategy and tactics), your age, strength, speed and reflexes. To reach a level to take on a person skilled with a knife takes years. You will need speed, power, agility, and correct techniques for unarmed gun or knife defense. In reality you will need to strike the attacker to "switch them off". And most people lack understanding of high quality striking techniques.

a. **Reality: It is always best to use a gun against an armed attacker.** You are much less likely to sustain any damage if you react to the attack quickly enough; your reaction was initiated when the person was far enough.

b. Use a blade if you don't have a gun. Only in a last-ditch effort use your hands against an armed attacker.

c. You increase your survivability when you use a weapon against an attacker instead of your hands. If you use your hands you will need to attack as much as possible with maximum aggression and striking areas that cause maximum damage (throat, groin, neck, joints, eyes etc.).

4. **You can train <u>low intensity</u> in your training environment and apply your tactics in a high intensity high threat environment**. This would be the equivalent of training by doing marathons in order to be good at sprints. This would clearly put you at a disadvantage as intensity affects the speed of movement which is more power orientated (more muscular contraction), as you move faster and the mind has to think/act faster which is a skill in itself. The way speed affects movement is that as muscles tense up it changes the arc and size of the moving parts of your body; it is easier to do a small movement fast than a large movement fast. The mind plays a huge role in speed of the movement and your ability to move fast.

a. **Reality:** You will likely die if you don't do high intensity training. Yes, for beginners you start off slowly to get the basics and mechanics correct. Then gradually increase the intensity of movements and scenarios. This applies both long term and short term. "Short term" means build up the intensity over a period of 30 minutes to 1 hour and "long term" is pushing a little harder over the period of 1 year.

b. You need to do it to increase your combat speed (especially your maximum pace) and this will also help your hand eye coordination at speed. Your mind gets used to the speed and the coordination becomes easier.

5. **You can learn 5 to 10 techniques in one day and then go out and remember them and apply them in a real situation.** This is the kind of training you might do on a short course of 2-3 days. If you do a short course, it's more advantageous to do *fewer techniques* and *learn them well* than to do many and not know any of them well. For instance, learning a particular weapon disarm for a whole day and make sure you fully understand as many aspects as possible before going on to the next technique. You can't be a pro athlete in a 3 days, 3 weeks or 3 months, so you can't be a deadly combatant either.

   a. **Reality:** It's only possible to learn well if the student goes off and trains the techniques on their own for a period of 6 months to 1 year or more. This is to make any technique a subconscious action without thought or deliberation.

   b. But even then, they will need *guidance* (technique correction) because doing repetitions of the wrong technique could be more damaging to their long-term training goals.

6. **You can do some half-hearted little punch in a close encounter as weapon retention and that will work in combat.** In reality, this type of striking will likely get you killed. *I see this a lot*, either due to misunderstanding of striking technique or misunderstanding of how hard you need to strike in close quarters to be victorious.

     a. **Reality:** To be effective you need to traumatize the attacker to the extent that they have a change of mind or they arc **incapacitated** for a long enough period of time to allow you to do something else, that might include a throat strike, groin kick or strike the back of the neck etc.

7. **Smooth is fast.** This might be good if you have a stack of 20 soldiers standing behind you to cover you, but this is not applicable in most combat situations. This is why we train speed (intensity specifically to reinforce neuromuscular (nerves in the muscles) pathways). Power movements speed up the mental aspects of hand eye coordination. Slow and deliberate training is only done in the initial phase of all training to make sure the students perform the technique properly, this could be 6 months to 1 year, then once the techniques are ingrained it's time for speed and intensity. As mentioned before, it's necessary to increase the intensity slowly.

     a. **Reality:** In combat, **fast is alive and slow is dead** (this must be balanced with control and accuracy and these two are controlled by realization and calm i.e., mindset). This doesn't mean you have to go so fast you lose control, but speed is very important and should be trained as an aspect of combat preparation. This is especially important if you are training for combat as an individual combatant.

<u>Important note:</u> Training for combat must always consist of all aspects of combat functions (purposes). Concepts such as physical exertion, mental aspect, tactics, and intensity and where possible a bit of chaos or "fog of war" (chaos with control) if that is possible. These allow the student to improve all areas that affect their performance in

a combat environment. You could see this as the prerequisites for all combat training including weapons type training such as rifle, pistol – even knife and unarmed training will use and perform with these aspects of combat. The lack of fitness, strength and *stamina* will always count against you in a combat situation if you lack any of these; this is why *keeping a basic standard of fitness is important.* For example, a 5km run 4-5 times per week with 2-3 sessions of full body calisthenics per week is a decent baseline of fitness.

Criteria for effective combat performance

These are some areas of physical performance criteria that need to be addressed to be effective in combat but this list is not exhaustive:

1. ***Speed:*** movement of the limbs and the forward or sideways movement of the whole body. The speed that you can move your limbs at is directly related to your strength and physical conditioning. You will never be able to move the upper body with maximum speed and efficiency if you don't have very good core strength. Specifically, your core muscles and or muscles of the torso, which would be but not limited to: external and internal obliques, transverse abdominis, rectus abdominis and the back muscles which support but not necessarily part of the initial of movement e.g., spinae erector muscles and quadratus lumborum.

2. ***Intensity:*** of the mind and body movement as a unit. This is both a mental and physical exercise as movement and speed with which your mind can function is related to the amount of intensity training you have done as the more intensity you do the faster your mind and body get as a coordinated unit, due to the conditioning of the muscles, ligaments and tendons. This is also related to and associated with the brain's ability to skip over the thinking process of the movement as it will become second nature once it is done enough times. This then allows the brain to focus on other aspects such as target acquisition and where to move as the body automatically accesses the weapon without a conscious thought process.

3. ***Muscle endurance:*** *the ability to lift a fairly light weight multiple times e.g.,* raising your rifle up to your shoulder 20 to 30 times will take muscles endurance. This is conditioned by doing high repetition weights or manual labor with fairly

light weights e.g., say your "1 repetition max" is 20 kg for your deltoid (shoulder muscle) then doing 3-5 sets of 20-30 reps with 5 kg will not build size but rather strength and endurance. Muscle endurance is more important for speed than heavy weights, as with heavy weights you build strength with too much mass, and mass can slow you down (harder for your body to move with the extra weight). Therefore, you want increased strength without too much mass to be efficient and stronger, pound for pound of muscles weight.

4. *Cardio fitness:* the ability to run for at least 30 minutes to 1 hour or more and to be able to function after the event. *Minimum* cardio you can do to still be fairly fit is 20 minutes 3 times a week, call this a baseline (minimum core fitness). To be reasonably cardio fit you could get away with doing 4 days of 30 minutes of running at a low intensity pace. To be combat fit you need to run at least 5 days a week 30 - 45 minutes at a time. Keep in mind rest is just as important as training hard because with no rest you will only break down. To take it to the next level you will need to add some speed training into the whole conditioning program. Speed increases your fitness quicker but can also bring on overtraining faster.

    a. The program will look something like this: Mon/Wed/Fri you can run in evenings 5 km (fairly hard run); Tuesday and Thursday morning do light 5 km run with 5-10 sprints in the evening.

    b. Muscular conditioning will look something like this: using 30-40 % of your maximum weight you do on Mon/Wed/Fri either after the run or in the morning, whole body conditioning. The sets can be anything from 2-5 sets (I would keep it to 2-3 sets), because you will do every major muscle group e.g., push up (bench press) uses all large pushing muscles: pecks, triceps and anterior deltoid. A pulling exercise such as chins (Latissimus pull down) will focus on most large muscles such as bicep, Latissimus, posterior deltoid (rhomboids and trapezius will be stabilizers). Pushing with the legs such as squats, done with the feet at different widths and feet at different angles, will work all large leg muscles such as rectus Femoris, vastus lateralis, or intermedius and Medialis. The number of reps will depend on the person's strength and conditioning and could vary from 10-20 repetitions and as high as 30 to 40 for well-conditioned athletes. Once again, don't go according to what others are doing – your genetic makeup is different and this is why you should go according to your own needs.

5. ***Timing:*** *this can apply to efficiency when changing a rifle magazine or watching the attacker and knowing when to counter* (both a physical and mental process as the body has to keep up with the mind). Timing is normally improved by repetitions as well as physical speed and power exercises. Let it happen – any thought process involved will slow you down, so just let it happen with a clear mind.

6. ***Balance:*** your ability to maintain equilibrium while moving, to maintain balance. This is normally a ***function of the core muscles*** and general muscle strength. Flexibility does help, and the ability to relax helps as the antagonistic muscles are more at rest than if they were tensed (as when doing a contraction). Use only the prime movers such as the quadriceps, and minimize the effect of the counter balancing muscles which would be the hamstring (also called the antagonistic muscles). Like any skill you want to develop,

doing more training in that discipline will help here so do exercises to improve your balance.

7. ***Core strength:*** in your stabilizing muscles, which also effects your balance, will also affect your ability to punch with power and how long you can carry a backpack, your running ability by stabilizing your hips during running, deadlift capacity and many other functions. Core strength is actually the core of all abilities when it comes to strength, agility and power (sprinting). Doing exercise such as hyperextensions and sit-ups help but are not specific core strength exercises. Deadlifts and planks will build the core more specifically.

8. ***Specific muscle development:*** weapon retention grip strength would be forearm muscles. These muscles as mentioned below can be strengthened by doing striking exercise and to build transverse abdominis, and obliques. Quadriceps and glutei muscles help for walking long distances. Sprinting uses mostly the gluteus and hamstrings as they are the "pull through" muscles. Spinae erector muscles are for backpacking, as well as rectus abdominis (stomach muscles).

9. ***Flexibility***: the ability of your limbs to do a large range of movement without stress and tension, that is within the body's natural range of maximum motion. The joints have a limit and should not be over stepped if you want good health, the legs have a ball and socket joint and any excessive range of motion can damage the edge of the joint. Flexibility allows ***fluid movement*** and ***prevents injury***. It also allows you to move fast in a more relaxed state and therefore helps with speed and execution of full techniques.

10. ***Repetition:*** of the correct technique, tactics and procedures with combat mindset done multiple times to the extent where the mind does not play a role in conscious thought of what to do in the action. Repetition allows the mind to work

on any little flaws in a given technique and strengthens the associated muscles. As time goes on and you do more repetitions your mind concentrates on your surroundings, as your hands and muscles start to react subconsciously.

The above are the physical aspects. You have to cater for the mental training as well, such as mental preparation in mindset and mental tools which deal with how your mind observes and processed the information in your environment. This includes the way you deal with the stress of combat, and is why it is imperative to include scenarios where stress is induced and the person is forced to overcome it:

How to teach weapons training for combat

One of the most important aspects to teach a student is how to teach themselves, this is the **introspective principal**. This demands confidence on the side of the student. They should learn from their mistakes and think about solutions to problems they find in training when confronted with them, and this will also help to develop a *flexible mind set for combat*. Most of my students that have trained for 2 or more years understand this principle and apply it when we train in class and this helps them to self-correct where their understanding allows. This is only possible if you have explained why certain techniques work and how they work so the person develops an understanding of the actual reasons for doing a technique or not.

This is master level understanding and is never taught or explained or even mentioned, this can lead to the situation sometimes phrased as "when the student is ready, the master will appear!" This is due to the fact the student has enough experience to draw from that allows them to decide if a certain change will be beneficial or not. This is limited to the extent where the student has either less of a capacity to be introspective and or the background knowledge to make a decision and whether this would be a better or not. This is directly proportional to the instructor's combat knowledge of real life combat and less of a fictional understanding.

The subject of street fighting/war/battle can be made more difficult to teach because of the amount of disinformation out there in the public domain. The student is presented with so many options, by this I mean systems, philosophies (view points) and instructors (with varied backgrounds and experience). Firstly, the systems are varied and numerous and not all geared towards practical application, this is borne out in reality when you have for instance a system like Capoeira being applied in MMA and the exponent loses, to a large extent it doesn't work in the street, the reason for this is the time it takes to execute most of the techniques which are large flowery movements that fit into a dance more than real combat. So a person without real combat knowledge but extensive training in Capoeira might be under the impression that his system is good for real street combat without having tested it (having a few street fights will quickly sort this self-deception out).

Some systems were originally practiced for real combat, and then they were adapted for sports purposes, which left them ***almost devoid of combative application***. This is one of the reasons so many different systems were tested in the MMA arena and some fell short and others grew in prominence. This doesn't mean all MMA fighting systems are applicable to the street because there are still rules in MMA and there are **no rules in the street**. This means in the street if a person grabs your arm for a lock, in MMA you can't punch them in the groin whereas in the street everything goes and this ***nullifies some of the techniques*** used in MMA, therefore some techniques that are effective in the MMA arena are not effective in the street. Another example of this would be in a close-up situation you are not allowed to head butt, but in the street this is a devastating strike and can win a fight with one strike.

This leads to a split in systems that use some aspects of fighting and ignore the rest. Some fighting systems, and this includes gun fighting systems, focus on the target shooting application of weapons training. This is important in combat but should be balanced with speed of shooting and intensity with the focus on both ***speed and accuracy and mobility.*** As with real street situations, you find yourself shooting at completely unique angles compared to your training if you do standard shooting training such as is done in any competition sport where the emphasis is on a standard shooting platform that might not even be possible to achieve in reality.

Some weapons fighting systems also only focus on the target practice aspect of pistol and leave out the close-in fighting that normally happens in self-defense situations, leaving it almost devoid of real-life application. Pistol or rifle training for combat has to take into consideration the **stress of combat** and chaos or dynamic nature where you don't know what the enemy is going to do. The chaos and dynamic nature create situations where you have to shoot in a stance you haven't trained, or in close confines such a small room or vehicle. It is also the timing of a confrontation which causes confusion to the operator and because you are not ready you tend to fumble or miss the mark due to time constraints imposed by the attacker. This also means a favorable stance can't always be achieved.

Then we have systems that are completely impractical for self-defense but the student will only realize this once they get into a situation and either lose the fight or get killed (so that's a bit too late to help). Systems that rely purely on brute force can be effective but might be limited in the situation where a bit of finesse is needed such as in a confrontation with a person with a knife and or gun. Having said that once you have managed to get into range of the attacker to manipulate the weapon from them, only brute force and or lethal application of force (throat strike) will persuade the person, a person doesn't just give up their gun or knife. This is why it's so important to strike them in an area that causes enough incapacitation that will encourage them to release the knife or gun.

Both the blade and handgun have certain basic principles that need to be applied to win against them and this also applies to the rifle. The pistol defense such as disarming a pistol requires you to control the barrel (this causes a stoppage) then you need to disable the attacker by a strike (normally a groin kick, throat strike or neck area in general) after the strike you can more easily use leverage to try manipulate the weapon from the attacker's hand. It doesn't have to be in this sequence

– you can strike as you grab the barrel, just don't lose the grip on the barrel before you have caused a stoppage.

The secret is it must be fast, aggressive and efficient, sometimes aggression can be the only thing you need but if the person is strong then you will need technique to win. If you are too close to the enemy then you can execute your disarm of his weapon system, if you are too far from them try the zig zag running technique. If you are far enough then run because at about 10 meters most average shooters cannot hit a running target specially one that is moving erratically, by this I mean side to side and up and down while running. This means the situation is dynamic if both the attacker and you are moving.

Then we have systems that rely on a **high level of skill** and manipulation of the weapon when trying to disarm the attacker. **The problem is trying to fit a slow technique that relies on fine motor skills** into an adrenaline pumping brute force attack at **high speed, it's just not going to work due to fine motor skills not working well when adrenaline is present.** This is one of the reasons Aikido doesn't work in the street. It might have stood a chance in the street if all your techniques were **practised at street combat speeds and intensity** with varied angles and direction of attack. But it isn't and therefore it can't be used in real combat because of the unrealistic speed of attack and the type of attacks which are done from way out of normal combat range, intensity and angles of attack etc.

You need to balance *skills* with both *brute force techniques*, and combine the ability to deal with the attacks that require a more delicate approach or fast light movements and attacks that require brute force; this is very difficult to teach and takes real skill and knowledge as an instructor.

As with all endeavours in life, there will be your academics and there will be warriors. Not **many people** have **the warrior spirit** and determination to be really good; most **are looking for a quick solution** (it does not exist, except in dreams and fantasy). Some are truly blessed to be both warriors and academically minded. Like with all sports or combat systems you have to **train hard** and **long** to be really good and if possible maintain them as they will deteriorate over time. Like with any sport or martial/fighting system, **the instructor's real-life experience** and understanding can accelerate learning or slow it down or even jeopardize the person's life as some systems will do due to their lack of real-life application.

When the student starts with their training, it is important to stress the *correct application of technique*, as this allows the student to **fight efficiently**. Efficiency is the key and that means your technique must be correct and to know what the correct techniques is you have to have experience and know how. It should also be noted that technique in the *wrong context* could also be lethal, so stress this aspect as well.

You also need to stress the **ability to move** as this is the basis of all forms of combat and those that can't move lack a major aspect of fighting ability which translates into fighting strategy and ultimately into victory.

The only time a gunfight is going to be static is when you *shoot from very long range*, or you *shoot from cover* such as in a dugout, or from a building, it could also be from a vehicle if used as cover but it only applies to where the engine is as the rest doesn't give much real ballistic cover. Otherwise in a battle or SHTF type situation you will most probably be in open patrolling, walking to an objective or moving by vehicle which is not good if attacked as vehicles don't offer much cover except for engine compartment etc.

Visualization techniques

These are a training aid and not essential to success.

This is not meditation; it's visualization of what you can do in a combat situation and the winning mindset. This **reinforces the winning attitude** and settles the technique in your mind so that you can fully apply the technique with mental understanding and physical preparation when you have done the necessary repetitions manually.

- Lie down in a relaxed environment.
- Breathe deeply and close your eyes.
- Consciously relax your muscles.
- Visualization should be realistic as in what is humanly possible, and systematic as in correct sequence of events.
- Realize that in reality you will have a certain amount of tension.
- There will be confusion in a fight, so picture yourself focusing, relaxing and working through it to prevail.
- You should see yourself drawing calmly, engaging each enemy as the situation presents itself, keeping all aspects of combat in mind, where the enemy is, the condition of your weapon, tactically who is the best person to engage first.
- Allow your mind to instinctively come to the correct conclusion. This is what your mind is more than capable of doing.
- Visualize as much detail as possible.

Stimulus and mental reaction programming

The student needs to develop an ability to overcome a natural fear response. This is done at different stages in the training. It replaces the normally fearful response with a confident one. This confident response is now part of the student's psychology, once they have got to a point where what previously used to scare them does not do so anymore.

Start with basic things, like showing the student a real blade, and ask them how it makes them feel. If they sense fear then they should breathe deeply and focus on the thoughts of confidence and winning and **righteous anger**. Righteous anger is only possible if you are righteous and in right standing with GOD.

This exercise can be done every few months or weeks, as often as the instructor feels it is necessary. It should be increased in complexity so that the student develops a mindset of winning and is able to stop the debilitating effects of fear.

Fear can slow you down, make you weak, and sometimes even completely immobilize you, so you need to work through these things in your mind, changing your attitude to one of confidence and strength (fortitude).

Even when the student thinks they have overcome those fears and have the winning mindset then it is still important to maintain their mental skill and to put them in a place of stress so they can strengthen their attitude.

Ask the student what creates a negative thought or fear for the student

1. It might be the sight of a blade
2. When the person sees a gun
3. It might be darkness and a strange person approaches them

4. Certain sounds, such as a gun cocking or a blade opening
5. It might be a person in the shadows with something in the hand (not necessarily a dangerous weapon).

This must then be overcome with a positive mindset through various exercises. This might take longer than you think as it takes a while to instill itself to where it becomes instinctive.

Summary of training principles

1. Teach only 1 or 2 techniques a day so the student can go off and learn/practise the subtleties at home, through repetition and using the introspective principle. If they don't have a lot of time at the training course to learn, then this can lead to problems if they do a technique incorrectly for too many repetitions as it could cause long term problems that will needed to be unlearned. Techniques have to be rehashed till the student understands it correctly.

2. Don't shoot lots of ammo, **do lots of technique** and **dry fire;** otherwise, it's a waste of money, time and energy. It is more advantageous to use less ammo and concentrate fully for 50 rounds worth of training than shoot 300 rounds and lose focus after just shooting 100 of them. A well-planned training program will cater for the basics which you should be good at for combat. This is magazine changes, stoppage drills, point aim and medium to long range shooting for combat, which would roughly be 100-300 meters which is what most combat ranges would be.

3. Explain, demonstrate and get the student to do the *technique slowly,*

    a. This is where you watch for any deviation from the technique. If you have explained it correctly then there won't be much deviation, you would also only add one new aspect at a time, minimizing mistakes.

    b. It would help to have the student be more *introspective* to learn from their mistakes and learn to adapt their technique as needed.

    c. As a training tool you can use video to show the person where they are going wrong, it's an excellent training tool I use it a lot.

4. Specific to combat is **movement training**, this is one of the most important aspects to teach to reach a really high level of combat efficiency and not necessary for sport shooting, unless the sport is a dynamic shooting discipline, probably like IDPA etc.

5. ***Correct repetition of good technique*** develops good shooting technique and fast access to this technique by your cerebellum. Sometimes called muscle memory, but probably has more to do with the neural pathways than muscles.

   a. These pathways are probably better developed than other neural pathways, the information to react and make the movement possible is also already established and easier to access. These pathways it seems can be improved and increased with use, correct nutrition and rest.

   b. Specific muscle development could also play a role as it takes very specific muscles to grip a weapon whether a handgun or rifle. These specific muscles need to strengthen and the ligament attachments for specific muscles also need to strengthen, and the combination of the specific strength and neural pathways having been established is what makes for the speed and accuracy. The muscles are primed and in peak physical conditioning allowing the body to use to their improved state to the utmost to achieve speed and accuracy.

   c. ***Efficiency of the techniques*** will also play a major role, developing and maintaining this is what matters. You want to be fast, accurate and move with efficiency, which means relaxed power in the case of striking and relaxed movement and accuracy in the case of shooting.

6. **Develop <u>intensity</u> slowly**, over months and if time allows **over years,** as this allows you to focus on your technique and *not lose your efficiency*. Efficiency is normally directly related to speed, so use the introspective principal to correct your technique. This is done by thinking through every step of the move you are trying to accomplish and self-correcting where necessary.

7. *Include stress* when the student has a *good grasp of the basics*. This may take up to 6 months to develop, not 6 days as some might think. This is contrary to what has been thought and indirectly believed for some time by many instructors, which is possibly brought about by the short course of 2-3 days being so numerous and prevalent in modern day teaching of any combat discipline.

   a. If you stress the student too early, they will subconsciously ingrain incorrect response and a breakdown of technique. This in turn will slow them down and make them less accurate than they should be, this is not so much a conscious thought but a subconscious one.

   b. When inducing stress do it *incrementally*, too fast and you break the person down, too slow and you take a vital aspect combat out of their grasp, affecting their combat efficiency.

   c. Monitor the student so you don't make it too hard, especially in the initial stages, as this causes a subconscious thought pattern that associates all combat with fear and trepidation as well as a weakening of the mind and body due to the over active adrenaline surge and body tensing up.

   d. Build it up to as close to real combat stress as possible but don't forget **SAFETY.** If done properly, this will take months if training weekends once a week for 2-4 hours. Like all things in life, the individual has a limited capability to adapt to stress, their upbringing will effect this to some extent as some individuals that are brought up in a tough environment will tend to be more resilient.

    e. Don't stress the student excessively without ***giving them the tools*** to deal/manage with the stress first. Teach them how to deal with the stress using mindset, this means the stress induced is only going to teach the person to lose control in the moment of combat if it is not accompanied by the tools to deal with them.

8. You have to include mindset and explain the importance of attitude and how being relaxed in a confrontation affects your performance. Constantly reinforcing the mindset is very important to performance in combat. Cultivating this is a long-term goal as it's not quick to change an ingrained mindset that took years to instill from youth. Only constant reinforcement will enable you to change this.

Practical Considerations For Rifle Training

Weapon safety

Safety with any weapon is primarily a <u>function of the mind</u> which means you either have a safety orientated mindset or you don't. The rifle being even more dangerous than a pistol because of the velocity of the bullet means it should be treated as very dangerous to the people standing around you great care should be taken with it. As with all weapons, knowing what is behind your target is important and even more so with a rifle because the velocity of a rifle bullet will be devastating at close and long range.

Major points to consider are:

    a. When handed a weapon, it is **your responsibility** to make it safe, that means anytime you are handed a weapon you can't rely on the fact the other person knew what they were doing or whether they understood safety protocol or not

        i. *Point in a safe direction*

        ii. Magazine out

        iii. Check mag well and chamber (these should be empty, no brass in the chamber)

        iv. Lower hammer

        v. Weapon is safe

    b. **Finger discipline**: keep your trigger finger off the trigger till you decide to engage a target. This is an easy technique, but it still needs to be applied by the mind which needs conditioning, after a few weeks it comes naturally if enforced correctly during training.

    c. **Engage the safety** when not shooting. This is more important during a training exercise than in combat because sometimes it is not appropriate to do in an environment where the enemy could literally be just around the corner.

    d. **Know what's behind your targets**, this would be especially pertinent for Close Protection officers and self-defense in the street. This might be very difficult to apply in a street confrontation as they sometimes occur very suddenly with no or little warning.

e. Watch your **muzzle discipline** especially when doing **team drills**. This becomes less applicable in real combat as you tend to run behind your team mates at times and therefore the finger discipline should be ingrained here and it's an expedient procedure to **lift the barrel** to point skywards (if you discharge the weapon while pointing up it won't normally kill or injure someone but if it pointed down and you discharge a round it can cause dangerous or fatal ricochets).

f. Always "make safe" before turning around to go back to the starting line of a range exercise. This obviously only applies to non-combat environment as you will always be "one up" (round in the chamber) and on safety in a combat situation.

Sighting in your weapon

Due to the numerous weapon sights out there and the many different types of scopes and sights available, it is not practical to deal with all of them in this manual. Basic principles will apply to the 'sighting in' of your weapon system. Any differences will arise due to the caliber and characteristics of the bullet which is determined by the bullet weight, ballistic coefficient, case and powder charge, length of projectile in comparison to its weight. The primer and primer hole size don't play such a major part for military type operations as the degree of accuracy is not needed as in precision shooting for competition.

Different calibers will have a different funnel of deviation that will keep the bullet in an approximately 4 inches funnel extending 50 meters out to about 300 meters. By funnel, we mean the bullet leaves the barrel and travels no higher than 2 inches and drops no lower than 2 inches, thus remaining within a 4 inch overall trajectory 'funnel'. A few examples would be the 5.6x45 caliber round which will drop quickly after 200 meters unless using a 75gr "boat tail" bullet design with a velocity greater than 3000 fps, which means the barrel length and twist rate will need to be commensurate with the bullet type. Cartridges like the 6.5x47 Lapua have good ballistic efficiency that can be used for long-range sniping, but for semi-auto rifles the cartridges are less capable at long range than for bolt-action rifles.

The problem will be the wind drift for a light bullet like the 5.56 caliber; it deviates easily because of the overall bullet weight. The 308 caliber drops off sharply after about 230 -250 depending on velocity and coefficient. Velocity is determined to some extent on the barrel length and powder charge.

Basic consideration for your iron sights

The sights can be adjusted in various ways. For example, on the LM/R4 (South African military rifle):

1. You adjust the front sight pin turning it so that it goes up or down that moves the barrel in the opposite way to the movement of the pin. This is for the distance adjustment, turning it in closer to the barrel will lift the barrel.
2. For lateral adjustment, you turn the screw on the side of the front sight and release the screw on the opposite side. If you move the pin to the left, you automatically move the barrel to the right.
3. If you are shooting too far left on the target then you have to move the front sight to the left to compensate. This will move the barrel to the right.

Basic considerations for scopes

If you want to use a scope then learn the characteristics of the individual scope you use. Know the limitations of the lenses. Prefer a **robust** scope or sights. Test all new equipment to the maximum extent to see if it loses its point of aim over time, especially with heavier calibers, and make sure it doesn't come loose on the mounts – use thread locker like Loctite, if it comes loose, or change your rings. If that doesn't work consider replacing it if you can afford to. You won't need more than 10x power magnification on a combat rifle like the M4, Galil, AK, and G3, FN or similar battle rifle.

Distance to set your weapon in

The best distance to set your sights in for a 223 caliber (5,56 x 45) NATO is at about 200-300 meters as this allows fast shots on target from 50 meters all the out to 400 meters. Which means the tunnel of accuracy for shooting is roughly maximum 4-5 inches high and 4 inches low at 300; this is a rough estimate the bullet velocity and trajectory will be different for each weapon system. So this is a rough guide to accuracy from close out to 300 meters. If you have a shorter barrel then you might be getting roughly 2700 - 2800 fps from a 12-inch barrel meaning you might want to set the zero range at about 200 meters and you'll have to compensate for more bullet drop at 300 meters.

Setting your sights for 0-200 meters

An alternative to the above 200-300 range setting is to sight the rifle in for 200 meters so you can engage an enemy or when hunting a quarry at ranges from 0-200 meters without too much calculation involved as the bullet flight path is flat, traveling between 2200-2800 fps even from a short barreled 223 caliber (5.56x45). The maximum height the path of the bullet will follow is 3-3.5 inches depending on the speed of the bullet and because it is zeroed at 200 meters it will be 'on' at 200 and no higher than 3 inches at 100 meters. The average person's head is approximately 8-10 inches so for headshots you'd keep the sights on the center of the head just where the mouth is and that should guarantee a hit between 0 and 200 meters.

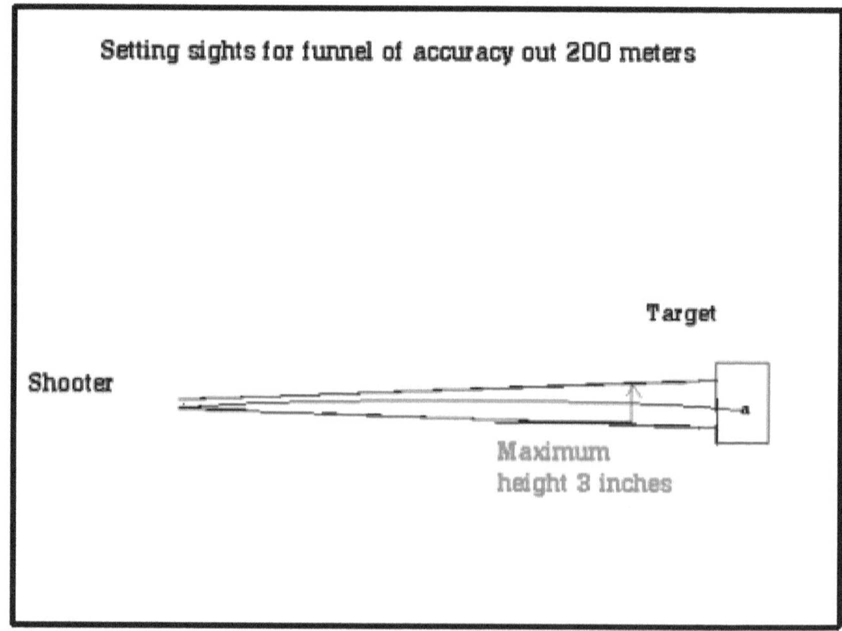

Weapon maintenance

The basics of weapons maintenance will apply to all rifles given commonality of working parts like barrel, sights, trigger mechanism with springs etc. Where possible the operators will be training on the system they will use in battle or on an operation, but as this will not always be possible, we will use a well-known design which stems from the German World War 2 design assault rifle (MP44) then copied by the Russians which was copied by the Israelis then reproduced by SA weapons manufacturers: the Galil, known in SA as the R4 or R5 or R6 depending on barrel length. The R4 has proven to be a reliable weapon, so we can deduce that the design by the Germans was an excellent design as the Galil and AK are based on the MP44 (Stumgewehr/ assault rifle).

Steps to follow:

1. Make the weapon safe.
2. Dismantle it per its manual of operations.
3. Clean off all dirt and carbon.
4. Wash down with liquid that dissolves oil and carbon, the weapon should be raw steal now.
5. Re-oil lightly for normal use (if you will be setting the weapon aside for months then oil liberally).
6. **Oil / grease heavily** for <u>sea</u> use: heavy oil application can cause a problem with dry sand blowing around so you will need to decide for yourself whether its viable for you to oil the weapon, it might not be needed for a short couple of hours of operating.
   a. Remember that *oil will come back at* you (you might get some in the face) if you use a suppressor, as will the hot gas, because the gas cannot escape forward out the barrel.
   b. Don't let it get sea sand in otherwise you will have major problem with some systems, as precision weapon parts don't do well with sand in them. If you want to use the weapon without oil for this reason, then wash thoroughly afterwards with soap and hot water then allow to dry completely and oil once dry.
7. Oil very *lightly,* or apply no oil for certain *desert terrain. You will still need to clean the weapon after every patrol or in the evenings depending on operational requirements and tactics and techniques* e.g., if you are patrolling in the desert but end up in towns where there is less dust to clog the weapon. Very little dust stays on a weapon if it it's got no oil on it.

Dismantling the rifle by feel

This is useful for night operations **or when you can't see** for some other reason.

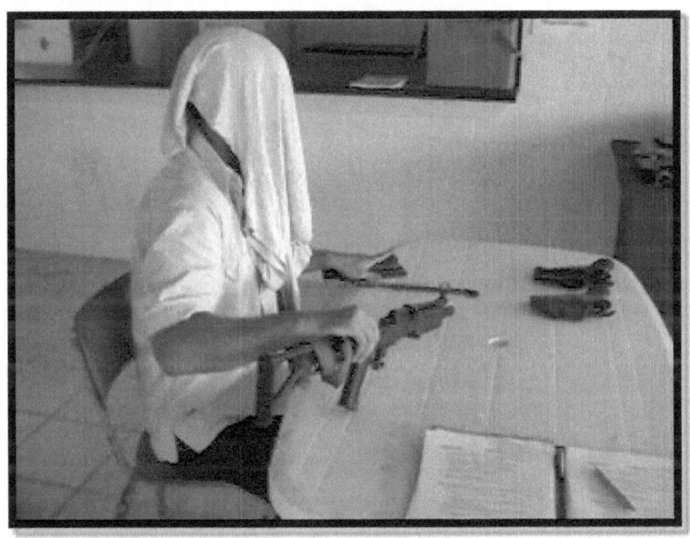

This exercise is done with a blindfold on so that it simulates doing a disassembly at night. The Elite operator might use this in a PSD situation or a military operation where cleaning and disassembly might be appropriate in low light.

The reason a person would disassemble a weapon at night is to clean it, so this can be quite an important skill, especially if the rifle you are using in a war zone needs a lot of attention such as the M16 or the FN FAL. Any precision weapon system needs more attention than something made with loose tolerances like the AK.

Special ranges

Try to use a range which has adequate shooting distances out to 300 meters as the semi auto 223 (5.56) has an effective range of approximately 300 meters. Training rooms for videos and lectures will be a benefit but not absolutely necessary. Having a room for night shooting where everything can be blacked out will be beneficial; facilities like this will most probably be on bigger, more professional ranges. Having a tower from which sniper over watch can be practiced would be advantageous but this is more likely for serious trainees, such as Close Protection teams, SWAT and military units.

A specific room for training hostage rescue scenarios will help for those wanting to develop these skills, which is more of a military or police function but can be trained by civilians if needed, as this can come in handy if your house is attacked by criminals and you need to clean it out a bit. Understanding "cornering" is essential here as exposing yourself too much can get you shot no matter how well trained you are.

Additional considerations will be steel (hardened) plates which are reactive, and if smaller in size they can provide a nice challenge to marksmanship skills. These plates are great for an indicator of hits as they make a sound when hit, and they don't need patching like paper targets do. Plates that can be reinstated by pulling a rope near you are going to speed things up and help for more time spent training. Sample options include:

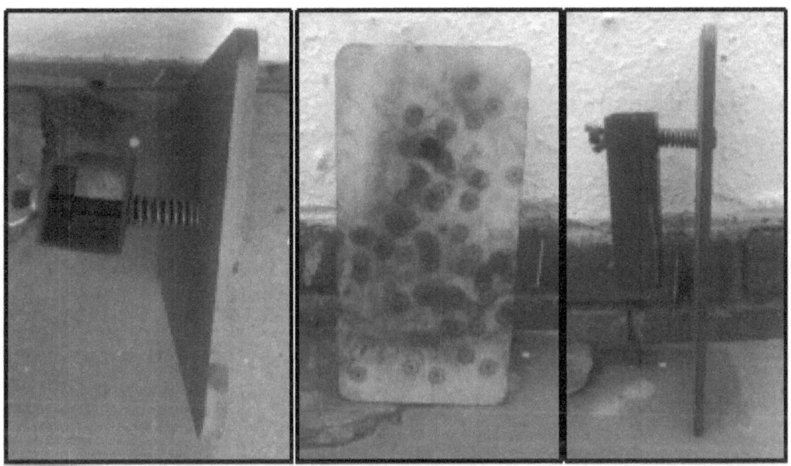

Having moving targets that can move across you from left to right or moving away or towards you is a great training aid but it not normally available because of the complexity and cost.

Medical kit

This should be obviously geared towards gunshot wounds. Therefore medical equipment such as Celox (blood coagulant), tourniquet (stops blood flow for major bleeds for artery), chest seal for serious torso wounds, and having the telephone number of closest hospitals with an emergency room for major trauma are a good idea. Most civilian ranges, especially the larger and heavily frequented ones will invariably have excellent medical services on standby, so check with range officials as applicable.

Bullet resistant vests

Having one on when doing team drills is a good idea as confusion and running across your team mate's firing line can result in a misunderstanding as accidents do happen. Especially high intensity training where speed and confusion are present.

Hearing protection

Hearing protection that cuts out loud sounds and allows you to hear are good to have but not essential. Electronic options are available that enable you to hear an instructor while still providing adequate sound protection. If you are worried about your hearing then use both ear plugs and muffs for double protection. Beware that gunshots are a lot more percussive in confined spaces such as "kill house" passages, especially with supersonic rifle ammunition (which almost all rifle ammo will be).

Folding knife

Having a folding knife comes in very handy as this can be used to cut targets off wooden frames/stands. There are many reasons to have a folder on you – this is expedient for general purpose, self-defense, weapon retention etc.

Training with your combat gear

Using your gear that you will be wearing in combat is a good idea to iron out all the problems that you don't want cropping up during combat. For example, once I was training with someone that had open magazine pouches. I mentioned that I didn't think they would work well. The person shrugged it off and ran and shot as they went. By the second or third barrier for cover he tried to reload only to find all his magazines lying on the ground.

You want to know what can stand up to the rigors of combat and what will be accessible or get in the way (or get snagged), such as webbing or rifle straps. This is important when seconds count – if a strap is in the way or causing you to slow down when looking for the rifle sights, that could get you killed.

Other aspects of testing your gear that will become apparent will be that velcro doesn't last as long as you would like, zips tend to wear out and stop functioning and then allow the webbing to open and this will allow the items to fall out. This is the same for clips that are made of plastic.

Basic Rifle Techniques

These are basic aspects of the fighting rifle you need to master above all else, in order to have a good chance of survival in combat. You could train more aspects of combat but complexity is not always the best approach because when it comes to combat it's the person who sees first, reacts fast and has the basic aspects of skills that allows them to win the fight who will prevail. To use a particular high dexterity complicated move, you would have to be in a situation that demands this, most street combat situation will be the same old stuff and calm focus and basic speed and accuracy will be adequate enough to prevail.

1. **Point aim**: is the instinctive ability ingrained by your training to be acted on without thought and still hit the target.

2. **Fast target acquisition**: means moving from target to target without thought or conscious action. This must be done to instinct and don't focus on a specific thought or action – just move from target to target as quickly as possible.

3. **Magazine changes**: should be done without thought and while moving, this means doing dry drills for 5 minutes every night from Monday to Friday. This done for 6 months will revolutionize your speed and efficiency. This is guaranteed if you follow that principle and stay consistent.

4. **Stoppage drills**: is the same as above with magazine drills, it becomes efficient and fast if done for at least 6 months. This I have done and it makes your magazine changes unconscious and leaves your mind open for tactical movement.

5. **Basic movement skills**: like your magazine changes and stoppage drills, will becomes second nature but this might be slightly more difficult as your body needs to first have the strength to do the actual drills.

6. **Mindset**: is not a physical skill but is probably the most

important aspect of combat training: This does take skill and dedication and should be applied when possible to all drills once the mindset is understood. This goes hand in hand with the actual physical exercises such as deep breathing.

To increase your survival with the above basic skills you will only need to perform the points mentioned with ever increasing speed and dexterity. Now for total mastery you add superior mindset and mobility and you will be a force to be reckoned with.

It goes without saying the weapon platform you are using must be reliable and in good working condition and maintained as such. This will take some dedication to find the right weapon for your use and purpose. Don't go for an expensive weapon prone to failure as this is about life and death and the firearm needs to be reliable, not beautiful.

Basics rifle fighting skills

Having covered the above skills focusing on basic weapon hand line, now we consider how to fight with the rifle:

1. **Weapon manipulation** skills as mentioned above.
2. **Shooting and movement**: this would include shooting on the move and or covering fire, which sometimes requires the operator to move to a position that allows them to give covering fire from an appropriate angle.
3. **Correct use of cover** will include but not limited to shooting around cover, best from of cover, moving from cover to cover. This can be difficult because most people that will do sports shooting will for the sake of efficiency lose respect for good cover and end up making bad cover practice and subconscious actions.
4. **Reaction to incoming fire** e.g., type of action (response) and speed of action (reflexes) and this could be to neutralize an attacker or attack the ambush itself.
5. **How to break contact** using assault and heavy fire on enemy and dissuade them from following and then attacking you again. This can but doesn't need to include anti tracking and E&E but those would be good skills to have too.
6. **How to stay calm when under fire**: this is the hardest to teach as it comes more from experience when in combat, having a good system of mindset training exercise can help but will have limited effect until you change

Don't miss out!

Visit the website below and you can sign up to receive emails whenever Mike Harland publishes a new book. There's no charge and no obligation.

https://books2read.com/r/B-A-BCLG-ITATB

BOOKS 2 READ

Connecting independent readers to independent writers.

Also by Mike Harland

Personal Security Detail Operations
Personal Security Detail Operations Book 1
Personal Security Detail Operations Book 2
Personal Security Detail Operations Book 3
Personal Security Detail Operations Book 4

The Fighting Rifle
The Fighting Rifle book 1
The Fighting Rifle Book 2
The Fighting Rifle Book 3

Standalone
Personal Protection And Body Guarding Manual